POWER PRAYERS

PRAYING GOD'S WORD FOR
BREAKTHROUGH

Steve Austin

Chosen
a division of Baker Publishing Group
Minneapolis, Minnesota

© 2025 by Stephen Austin

Published by Chosen Books
Minneapolis, Minnesota
ChosenBooks.com

Chosen Books is a division of
Baker Publishing Group, Grand Rapids, Michigan

Printed in the United States of America

All rights reserved. No part of this publication may be reproduced, stored in a retrieval system, or transmitted in any form or by any means—for example, electronic, photocopy, recording—without the prior written permission of the publisher. The only exception is brief quotations in printed reviews.

Library of Congress Cataloging-in-Publication Data

Names: Austin, Steve, author
Title: Power prayers : praying God's word for breakthrough / Steve Austin.
Description: Minneapolis, Minnesota : Chosen, a division of Baker Publishing Group, [2025]
Identifiers: LCCN 2025002672 | ISBN 9780800773380 paperback | ISBN 9780800778309 casebound | ISBN 9781493452286 ebook
Subjects: LCSH: Prayer—Christianity
Classification: LCC BV210.3 .A927 2025 | DDC 248.3/2—dc23/eng/20250616
LC record available at https://lccn.loc.gov/2025002672

Unless otherwise noted, all Scripture is taken from the New King James Version®. Copyright © 1982 by Thomas Nelson. Used by permission. All rights reserved.

Scripture marked AMP are taken from the Amplified® Bible, Copyright © 2015 by The Lockman Foundation. Used by permission. lockman.org

Scripture marked AMPC taken from the Amplified® Bible, Copyright © 1954, 1958, 1962, 1964, 1965, 1987 by The Lockman Foundation. Used by permission. lockman.org

Scripture quotations marked CSB have been taken from the Christian Standard Bible®, copyright © 2017 by Holman Bible Publishers. Used by permission. Christian Standard Bible® and CSB® are federally registered trademarks of Holman Bible Publishers.

Scripture quotations marked ESV are from The Holy Bible, English Standard Version® (ESV®), copyright © 2001 by Crossway, a publishing ministry of Good News Publishers. Used by permission. All rights reserved. ESV Text Edition: 2016

Scripture quotations marked HCSB are from the Holman Christian Standard Bible®, copyright © 1999, 2000, 2002, 2003, 2009 by Holman Bible Publishers. Used by permission. Holman Christian Standard Bible®, Holman CSB®, and HCSB® are federally registered trademarks of Holman Bible Publishers.

Scripture quotations marked KJV are from the King James Version of the Bible.

Scripture quotations marked MSG are taken from *The Message*, copyright © 1993, 2002, 2018 by Eugene H. Peterson. Used by permission of NavPress. All rights reserved. Represented by Tyndale House Publishers.

Scripture quotations marked NASB taken from the (NASB®) New American Standard Bible®, Copyright © 1960, 1971, 1977, 1995, 2020 by The Lockman Foundation. Used by permission. All rights reserved. www.lockman.org

Scriptures marked NIV taken from the Holy Bible, New International Version®, NIV®. Copyright © 1973, 1978, 1984, 2011 by Biblica, Inc.® Used by permission of Zondervan. All rights reserved worldwide. www.zondervan.com. The "NIV" and "New International Version" are trademarks registered in the United States Patent and Trademark Office by Biblica, Inc.®

Scripture quotations marked NLT are taken from the *Holy Bible*, New Living Translation, copyright © 1996, 2004, 2015 by Tyndale House Foundation. Used by permission of Tyndale House Publishers, Carol Stream, Illinois 60188. All rights reserved.

Scripture quotations marked TPT are from The Passion Translation®. Copyright © 2017, 2018, 2020 by Passion & Fire Ministries, Inc. Used by permission. All rights reserved. ThePassionTranslation.com.

This publication is intended to provide helpful and informative material on the subjects addressed. Readers should consult their personal health professionals before adopting any of the suggestions in this book or drawing inferences from it. The author and publisher expressly disclaim responsibility for any adverse effects arising from the use or application of the information contained in this book.

Cover design by InsideOut Creative Arts, Inc.

Baker Publishing Group publications use paper produced from sustainable forestry practices and postconsumer waste whenever possible.

CONTENTS

Foreword   11
Introduction   13
Praying Power Prayers   17

I. Relationship with God

1. Prayer of Salvation   35
2. Prayer of Rededication   36
3. Prayer to Receive God's Love   37
4. Prayer of Repentance   38
5. Prayer of Surrender   39
6. Prayer to Put God First   41
7. Prayer to Abide in Christ   42
8. Prayer for Deeper Walk with God   43
9. Prayer to be Holy   44
10. Prayer to be More Christlike   45
11. Prayer to Walk in the Holy Spirit   46
12. Prayer to Hear the Voice of God   47
13. Prayer of Thanksgiving   49

14. Prayer of Praise 50
15. Prayer to Trust God More 51
16. Prayer for More Faith 53
17. Prayer for Obedience 54
18. Prayer for Fresh Fire 55

II. Relationship with Others

19. Prayer to Walk in Love 59
20. Prayer for Friendship, Community 60
21. Prayer for Single Person Desiring a Mate 61
22. Prayer for Wisdom, Discernment with People 63
23. Prayer for Favor with People 64
24. Prayer to Avoid or Resolve Conflict 65
25. Prayer to Restore Relationship 66

III. Personal Prayers

26. Prayer for the Year 71
27. Prayer for a Blessed Week 72
28. Prayer Against Deception 74
29. Prayer for Breakthrough 75
30. Prayer to be a Great Life Manager 76
31. Prayer for More Discipline 78
32. Prayer for Wisdom 80
33. Prayer to Know God's Will, Guidance 81
34. Prayer for Favor 82
35. Prayer for Joy 83
36. Prayer for Peace 84
37. Prayer to Manage Thought Life 85
38. Prayer of Protection 87
39. Spiritual Warfare Prayer 89

40. Prayer to Live a Purpose-Driven Life   90
41. Prayer to Represent Jesus Well   92
42. Prayer to Live the Abundant Life   93
43. Prayer for Expansion   94
44. Prayer to be a Better Time Manager   95
45. Prayer When Walking Through a Trial   96
46. Prayer for Hope, Encouragement   97
47. Prayer to Let Go of the Past   98
48. Prayer When You Feel Overwhelmed   99
49. Prayer When You Feel Weary, Burned Out   101
50. Prayer for Rest   102
51. Prayer When You're Waiting   103
52. Prayer to Take Care of Your Temple   104
53. Prayer over Your Home, Property   106
54. Prayer for Good Sleep   107
55. Prayer for Move, Transition   109
56. Prayer for Upcoming Travels   110
57. Prayer for Purchase of Home   112
58. Prayer for Sale of Home   113

IV. Marriage and Family

59. Prayer for Your Marriage   117
60. Prayer for Wife to Pray   118
61. Prayer for Husband to Pray   120
62. Prayer for Healthy Pregnancy   122
63. Prayer for Your Children   123
64. Prayer to Dedicate Child   124
65. Prayer for Wayward Child   126
66. Prayer for Wayward Spouse   127
67. Prayer for Unsaved Spouse   128

68. Prayer for a Troubled Marriage   130
69. Prayer for Unsaved Family Members   131
70. Prayer for Family Reconciliation, Peace, Unity   133

V. Finances and Career

71. Prayer for Finances   137
72. Prayer for Financial Wisdom, Stewardship   138
73. Prayer over Tithes and Offerings   140
74. Prayer to Pay Off Debt   141
75. Prayer for Restoration After Financial Loss   143
76. Prayer for Investments   144
77. Prayer for a Job   146
78. Prayer for Favor, Promotion at Work   147
79. Prayer for Peace, Protection at Work   148
80. Prayer to Start a Business   149
81. Prayer over Existing Business(es)   151

VI. Healing the Body

82. General Prayer for Healing   155
83. Healing from Cancer   157
84. Prayer for Cancer Treatment   159
85. Healing from Heart Disease   160
86. Healing from High Blood Pressure   161
87. Healing from Diabetes   163
88. Healing from Neurological Disorders   165
89. Healing from Respiratory Disorders   167
90. Healing from GI Disorders   168
91. Healing from Pain   170
92. Healing from Female Problems   171
93. Healing from Male Problems   173

94. Healing from Infertility   174
95. Healing from Stroke   176
96. Healing from Eye, Sight Problems   177
97. Healing from Ear, Hearing Problems   179
98. Prayer for Wisdom in Health-Care Decisions   181
99. Prayer Before a Medical Test   182
100. Prayer Before a Medical Procedure   183
101. Prayer for Doctors, Nurses, Other Care Providers   184
102. Prayer for Another Person's Healing   185

VII. Healing the Soul

103. General Prayer for Healing the Soul   189
104. Prayer of Forgiveness   190
105. Healing from Abandonment   192
106. Healing After Abortion   193
107. Healing from Abuse   195
108. Healing from Adultery   197
109. Healing from Betrayal   198
110. Healing After Divorce   200
111. Healing from Grief   201
112. Healing After Loss of Loved One   203
113. Healing After Miscarriage   205
114. Healing from Rejection   206
115. Healing from Sexual Assault   207
116. Healing from Trauma   209

VIII. Freedom

117. General Prayer for Freedom   213
118. Freedom from Addiction   214

119. Freedom from Anger 216
120. Freedom from Anxiety 218
121. Freedom from Bitterness 219
122. Freedom from Comparison 221
123. Freedom from Criticalness 222
124. Freedom from Depression 223
125. Freedom from Disappointment 225
126. Freedom from Eating Disorders 227
127. Freedom from Fear 229
128. Freedom from Guilt, Shame, Condemnation 230
129. Freedom from Insecurity 231
130. Freedom from Lack, Poverty 232
131. Freedom from Loneliness, Isolation 234
132. Freedom from Mental Torment, Suicidal Thoughts 236
133. Freedom from Negativity 237
134. Freedom from Panic Attacks 239
135. Freedom from Pride 240
136. Freedom from Procrastination 241
137. Freedom from Selfishness 243
138. Freedom from Self-Pity, Victim Spirit 244
139. Freedom from Self-Sabotage 245
140. Freedom from Sexual Immorality 247
141. Prayer to Break Generational Curses 249
142. Prayer to Break Word Curses 250
143. Prayer to Break Soul Ties 251

FOREWORD

I AM SO HAPPY about Steve Austin's new book *Power Prayers* and all the ways it will transform lives. I've known Steve for twenty-five years, and I think he is brilliant! He and I do a monthly healing service together on Zoom, and I am always amazed by his deep knowledge of the Word of God, the countless people he prays for, and the many miracles he sees.

Steve's books help people gain knowledge and love for God's Word. *Power Prayers* will also help you pray effectively according to God's Word, which is one of the most important things we can do in life. When you pray the Scripture-based prayers in this book, you can have confidence and peace that God will respond mightily to your prayers. Whatever your need is, there is a prayer to cover it in this book!

I have experienced the awesome power of prayer throughout my life. When our daughter Lisa was born, the umbilical cord was wrapped around her neck, and we were told she might never walk or talk. We didn't expect that news, but we sought God and prayed, and He did a miracle and healed her. She has been a great minister and preacher for decades and is so healthy and strong. God is a miracle-working God, and He never changes!

In 1981, I was diagnosed with metastatic liver cancer and given a few weeks to live. There was no hope in the natural, but God is a supernatural God. He can do things doctors and medicine can't. We stood on God's Word, which cannot fail, every day—praying and declaring it with faith. It wasn't easy. I got down to eighty-nine pounds, and I was so weak at times. I had to fight the good fight of faith and refuse to give up. But God came through and wiped out every trace of cancer from my body. Today, I am ninety-two years old and still going strong.

If you are battling cancer or any other disease, you can be sure that God's Word says He heals us of all our diseases (Psalm 103:2–3). What a great promise! God always keeps His Word. When you pray His Word back to Him, He watches over it to perform it, and it will not return to Him void! *Power Prayers* will help you to do just that. It can save your life.

Dodie Osteen,
cofounder of Lakewood Church, author

INTRODUCTION

ARE YOU READY to supercharge your prayers and see God move in your life like never before? In this book, I am going to give you the biblical keys to praying powerful prayers that get results and provide you with 143 Scripture-based prayers covering every aspect of your life. When you pray effectively, it will change your life. You will see God respond to your prayers like never before and experience new levels of His favor, blessings, and victory.

Every time you pray, you are connecting with the God of the universe, who has all power and wisdom. When God told Moses, "I AM WHO I AM," He was saying, "I am everything: your healer, deliverer, provider, protector, counselor, strengthener, and comforter. I am whatever you need me to be" (see Exodus 3:14). He is the source of everything you need and has the solution to every problem you face.

You are God's child, and He has great plans for your life. He said, "I know the plans I have for you . . . plans to prosper you and not to harm you, plans to give you hope and a future" (Jeremiah 29:11 NIV). These plans are birthed through prayer. God does very little on the earth without prayer, as I explain in the first chapter. As you pray the prayers in this book with faith, you can be confident that they are hitting the mark because they are based on God's own Word—and His Word never fails!

I was inspired to write this book because the number one comment I got from my first book, *God Heals*, was people saying how much they loved the prayers. One lady translated the *Prayer for Sleep* into Spanish for her mother in Mexico who suffered from insomnia. She was instantly delivered and has slept like a baby ever since. A man gave the same prayer to his wife, who struggled with insomnia, and she also was instantly delivered. People have written to me saying that they were healed of various diseases, and they saw pain leave their bodies after praying the prayers in that book. Others asked if they could copy the prayers and give them to friends and family. People come up to me all the time at church and say, "You may not remember me, but you prayed for me a while back, and I received healing, or I got the job, or my marriage was restored."

My secret is simple: I pray the Word of God with faith and fervency. I remind God of His Word and believe to the core of my being that He will answer my prayers. I didn't always pray and have faith like this, but I have grown over the years—and you can too!

I have been a fervent prayer warrior and student of prayer for over thirty years, and I've been privileged to pray for tens of thousands of people. I have seen God do astonishing things in response to prayer—tumors vanish, people set free from addictions and other strongholds, financial miracles, wayward children and spouses turn around, broken marriages restored, and countless other miracles and breakthroughs. Prayer is an exciting, grand adventure connecting with the God of the universe and seeing Him respond.

In the first chapter, I share some insights about the importance and power of prayer and give you tips on how to pray more effectively. But the real stars of this book are the 143 Scripture-based power prayers. The prayers are divided into eight categories:

1. Relationship with God
2. Relationship with Others

3. Personal Prayers
4. Marriage and Family
5. Finances and Career
6. Healing the Body
7. Healing the Soul
8. Freedom

If you don't see a prayer for your specific need, there is a general prayer in each section that you can adapt to your situation. There are, for example, 21 prayers in the "Healing the Body" section. If you don't see a prayer for your ailment, you can use the "General Prayer for Healing" and plug your ailment into that prayer.

I encourage you to make these prayers your own. They are a great foundation based on God's Word, but since I don't know your exact situation, please add your own requests and details to them as needed. As you pray them, God may bring other verses or prayer points to your mind. Since these prayers are Scripture-based, they are also a great way to renew your mind with what God's Word says about your situation. Each prayer is followed by a list of verses used in the prayer, providing a convenient Scripture guide for each prayer topic that you can use for self-study and reflection.

You may need to stack several of these prayers and pray them often to get the victory in your situation. Prayer and faith don't always work instantly like a magic wand. We must persevere, especially with things like generational curses, soul traumas, addictions, strongholds, and serious trials. It is usually necessary to hit those repeatedly in prayer before getting the ultimate victory. I've experienced instant results many times, and I never limit God, but most of the time ultimate victory requires being intentional and persistent in prayer.

I am so excited about what God is going to do in your life and the lives of everyone for whom you pray. Get your faith and expectancy up! God is taking you from glory to glory. Armed with *Power Prayers*, you're about to see new levels of victory in your life! Let's go!

PRAYING POWER PRAYERS

IT IS NOT HYPERBOLE to say that prayer is one of the most important things we can do in life. What could be more important than connecting with the God of the universe? More thrilling than praying for yourself and others and seeing God answer in miraculous ways? More consequential than partnering with God Almighty to pray His will through on the earth? That's why the apostle Paul told us to pray without ceasing. It's also why the devil tries everything he can to hinder, distract, discourage, and disrupt our prayer life. He doesn't want us to have intimacy with God, hear from Him, or use the power of our prayers. He knows the awesome power of prayer better than most Christians do. In this chapter, I want to share some insights about the importance and power of prayer and biblical keys to praying effective prayers that get results.

The Supreme Importance of Prayer

Jesus said, "My house shall be called a house of prayer" (Matthew 21:13). He could have said many other things about His house. "My house shall be called a house of worship." That's certainly important. "My house shall be called a house of evangelizing the lost, teaching, fellowship, service." All of these things are vitally important. But the one thing Jesus highlighted was *prayer*. He was saying, "Of all the things you do in church, prayer is the most important because it is the foundation for everything else." Prayer is our spiritual lifeblood as believers, and it connects us to God more than anything else. We can connect to Him through worship, His Word, His creation, and many other ways. But prayer is an ongoing dialogue with God and the primary way we have intimate fellowship with Him and involve Him in our lives. It also gives Him permission to intervene in our lives and the lives of those we pray for.

Jesus not only called the church a "house of prayer," singling out prayer over other church activities, He demonstrated the preeminence of prayer in His own life. The verses below give us a snapshot of how devoted Jesus was to prayer:

- "He Himself often withdrew into the wilderness and prayed" (Luke 5:16).
- "Now in the morning, having risen a long while before daylight, He went out and departed to a solitary place; and there He prayed" (Mark 1:35).
- "And when He had sent the multitudes away, He went up on the mountain by Himself to pray" (Matthew 14:23).
- "Now it came to pass in those days that He went out to the mountain to pray, and continued all night in prayer to God" (Luke 6:12).
- "And when He had sent them away, He departed to the mountain to pray" (Mark 6:46).

We see from these verses that even though Jesus was the Son of God, He prioritized prayer as a nonnegotiable in His life. He was busier than you and I will ever be, with throngs of people following Him everywhere, multitudes to teach and minister to every day, jealous religious leaders to contend with, and disciples to lead. Yet, He always made time to pray and connect with the Father. We are told that He prayed all night, woke up well before daylight to pray, and often withdrew to a solitary place to pray.

It begs the question: *If Jesus, who was God in the flesh, needed to pray this much, how much more do we?* Is there anything more important than connecting with the God of the universe? Like Jesus, we need to prioritize prayer and pray throughout the day, not just keep it in a morning "quiet time" box. If we can check our phones all day, surely we can pray to the God of the universe throughout the day. I've heard people say, "I'm too busy to pray." I say this respectfully, but if you are too busy, distracted, tired, or whatever to pray, something needs to change. A prayerless Christian is a powerless, rudderless Christian.

The apostle Paul wrote that we should "pray without ceasing" (1 Thessalonians 5:17). Prayer is the only thing the Bible explicitly tells us to do without ceasing. Does this give us an idea of how important prayer is? Paul said we should do it nonstop. He also instructed us to "pray in the Spirit *on all occasions with all kinds of prayers and requests*" (Ephesians 6:18 NIV, emphasis added). In other words, pray all the time about everything. In Philippians 4:6, he added, "Don't worry about anything; instead, *pray about everything*" (NLT, emphasis added). Prayer is our first and best resort, not a Hail Mary last resort when everything else has failed. It should be our automatic first response to everything. God doesn't want us to just pray about the big things or when we are in trouble. He wants us to *pray about everything*. Scripture says that He has numbered the hairs on our head, so there is nothing too trivial to pray about (see Matthew 10:30). He wants to be intimately involved in every aspect of our lives.

I pray first thing every morning during my devotional time.

I pray throughout the day.

I pray on my morning walk.

I pray in the shower.
I pray in the car.
I pray before and often during meetings.
I pray at the gym.
I pray before bed.
Prayer is an integral part of my daily life.

I even pray in my sleep many times. If you do this, too, you get it. I'll be halfway sleeping and praying during the night if I feel a burden to pray for something.

I'm not telling you this to impress you, and I don't do it as a religious task. Prayer is about relationship, not religion. And I don't float around on a cloud all day praying. I have a lot of responsibilities and challenges like everyone else. But I'm here to testify that it is possible to pray without ceasing as we go about our daily tasks. As my walk with the Lord has grown deeper and more intimate over the years, I have loved having constant fellowship with Him.

I realize how much I desperately need God. I need His grace. I need His wisdom. I need His guidance. I need His strength. I need His protection. I need His anointing to do what He's called me to do. I need His help living the Christian life in this world. I need His healing for my body and soul. I need everything He has for me. I used to be prideful when I was a young attorney. I had an independent "I've got this" spirit. But as I matured, I realized that I don't want to do anything apart from Him. Why would I? He makes everything better and helps me in every way. I want Him involved in every aspect of my life all the time.

If you are married, I encourage you to pray with your spouse every day. There are many ways we connect with our spouse—mentally, emotionally, physically, recreationally—but the deepest and most meaningful way is spiritually. That's because our spirit is the deepest part of our being. When you and your spouse connect spiritually every day, you will form the deepest, most unbreakable bond. My wife and I have had a devotional time together every morning of our thirty-year marriage for at least an hour, sometimes two to three hours on days off from work. It is not a set format. I don't believe in making our devotional time formulaic because it can become a lifeless, robotic ritual.

I believe a devotional time should be dynamic and Spirit-led. We take turns praying out loud for ourselves, other people, and many other things. We read our Bibles. We share revelations and prophetic dreams God has given us. We say Scripture declarations over ourselves and our children. We give thanks and praise to God. We do spiritual warfare. There is a lot packed into that hour. Even if we have had an argument the night before, we meet in the prayer room without fail to forgive each other, repent, and start afresh. This devotional time has been the anchor of our marriage. When life has thrown us curveballs and it's gotten rough, our time together with God every morning has helped us overcome every adversity. Through every storm, our anchor has held beyond the veil (see Hebrews 6:19).

The Awesome Power of Prayer

James 5:16 says, "The effective, fervent prayer of a righteous man avails much." Notice, it is "a righteous man," meaning one. It doesn't have to be two or three or a whole group of people. God doesn't need numbers. Just one righteous person's prayers avail much. You need to know that *your own prayers avail much*. That means they accomplish much and have tremendous power.

The next two verses say, "*Elijah was a man with a nature like ours, and he prayed earnestly that it would not rain; and it did not rain on the land for three years and six months. And he prayed again, and the heaven gave rain*" (James 5:17–18, emphasis added). God was very deliberate about everything He put in His Word. He wanted us to know that the great Elijah had a nature just like ours. The great heroes of the Bible were not superhuman. They had weaknesses and made mistakes just like us. Abraham lied about Sarah and slept with her maid. Moses killed an Egyptian. David committed adultery with

Bathsheba and had her husband killed. Elijah fell into depression and asked God to take his life. Peter cut off a man's ear and publicly denied Jesus three times. Paul persecuted Christians and consented to the murder of Stephen. Still, God used them tremendously, and their prayers were powerful. He wanted to convey to us in the clearest way that these heroes were just like you and me, and our prayers can be just as powerful. Don't ever allow your weaknesses, mistakes, and failures to cause you to pray insecure, weak prayers. You are a blood-bought, blood-washed child of the Most High God, and your prayers are more powerful than you can fathom.

My favorite example in the Bible of how powerful one person's prayers can be is found in Ezekiel 22:

> "The people of the land have used oppressions, committed robbery, and mistreated the poor and needy; and they wrongfully oppress the stranger. *So, I sought for a man* among them who would make a wall, and stand in the gap before Me on behalf of the land, that I should not destroy it; but I found no one. *Therefore* I have poured out My indignation on them; I have consumed them with the fire of My wrath; and I have recompensed their deeds on their own heads," says the Lord God.
>
> Ezekiel 22:29–31 (emphasis added)

This was God Almighty saying He sought for one person who would "stand in the gap"—meaning to pray and intercede—on behalf of the land. He didn't say He sought a prophet, an apostle, or other spiritual heavyweight. He just sought for one person who would pray. One person could have made all the difference in the entire land. That's how powerful your prayers are! Your prayers could literally make the difference in your family, workplace, city, country, even the world. But God could not find a single person who would intercede, because everybody was busy, distracted, on their phones, and consumed with their own affairs. *Therefore*, He had to pour out His judgment on the land.

Why would the God of the universe, who has all power and can do whatever He wants, seek for a man to pray? Because God chose to give man dominion in the earth realm and partner with him to bring about His will on earth. When God created man, He said four very powerful words: *"Let them have dominion"* (Genesis 1:26, emphasis added). Psalm 8:6 says, "You have made him [man] to have dominion over the works of Your hands; You have put all things under his feet." Psalm 115:16 adds, "The heaven, even the heavens, are the Lord's; but *the earth He has given to the children of men*" (emphasis added). So, God has given us dominion in the earth realm and partners with us to bring about His will on earth. That's why the Bible calls us "God's fellow workers" and "workers together with Him" (1 Corinthians 3:9; 2 Corinthians 6:1).

We are God's partners on earth. Besides certain things He does sovereignly, God does very little on the earth without somebody praying and agreeing with His will. Watchman Nee explained this perfectly in his book *Let Us Pray*. He said that God's will is like a powerful locomotive, but our prayers are the tracks upon which that locomotive runs.* Without our prayers, the locomotive won't go anywhere. This is very important to understand. God may want to do something, but as we saw above in the Ezekiel 22 passage, if no one bothers to pray, it will likely not happen. That's why it is so important that we pray about everything. Prayer is about so much more than getting our own needs met. God has chosen to work through our prayers to manifest His will on the earth. Our prayers have tremendous power to impact people, the world, and whatever the Holy Spirit prompts us to pray about.

Jesus made some audacious promises regarding the power of our prayers:

- "Ask, and it *shall* be given you" (Luke 11:9 KJV, emphasis added). I love this verse for its clear-cut simplicity. Jesus said

---

*Watchman Nee, *Let Us Pray* (New York: Christian Fellowship Publisher, Inc., 2014) 159.

just ask and it will be given to you. Conversely, James 4:2 says, "You do not have because you do not ask." So, God beckons us to ask. I wonder how many blessings people have missed out on because they simply didn't ask.

- "Whatever you ask the Father in My name He will give you" (John 16:23).
- "If you abide in Me, and My words abide in you, you will ask what you desire, and it shall be done for you" (John 15:7).
- "Whatever things you ask in prayer, believing, you will receive" (Matthew 21:22).

These are red-letter Jesus words. Do we really believe them? Do we really expect that if we ask God for anything in faith, He will give it to us? I want to stir you up today to believe God and pray big, bold prayers. God honors big, bold prayers because big, bold prayers honor Him. He's the God of the universe. He's a great, big, mighty God who has all power, and you are His beloved child. He made you thousands of amazing promises in His Word, covering every aspect of your life, and all of His promises are "Yes" and "Amen" in Christ Jesus (see 2 Corinthians 1:20). I included several of them in each prayer in this book. Dare to ask and believe Him for them!

Three Keys to Praying Power Prayers

Now that we have looked at the supreme importance and awesome power of prayer, I want to walk you through three simple keys to praying power prayers that get results. Every believer has equal access to God through prayer. God doesn't have favorites. The Bible says every believer can have boldness to enter His presence by the blood of Jesus (see Hebrews 10:19–22).

We all have equal access, but not all prayers are equal. Some prayers are effective, and some are not. James 5:16 tells us, "The effective, fervent prayer of a righteous man avails much." Notice it is *effective* prayers that avail much. God did not slip that word in there by accident. The word *effective* means by implication that there are also *ineffective* prayers.

Jesus' disciples grew up in good Jewish homes where prayer was practiced, but apparently their prayers weren't as effective as they had hoped. They approached Jesus while He was praying and said, "Lord, teach us to pray" (Luke 11:1). If the disciples were already praying effectively and getting results, they wouldn't have needed to ask Jesus how to pray. This request alone tells us there are effective and ineffective ways to pray.

Many Christians pray ineffective prayers because they pray according to their religious tradition or their own mind instead of how the Bible teaches us to pray. The Bible gives us three essential components of effective prayers—what I call power prayers:

1) Based on God's Word
2) Prayed with faith
3) Prayed with persistence

Based on God's Word

The first key to praying power prayers is that they are *based on God's Word*. First John 5:14–15 says, "Now this is the confidence that we have in Him, that if we ask anything according to His will, He hears us. And if we know that He hears us, whatever we ask, we know that we have the petitions that we have asked of Him." This verse says we can have absolute confidence that when we pray according to God's will, He not only hears us but will grant our petitions. How do we know we are praying according to God's will? By praying His Word. His written Word spells out His will.

God's Word is His covenant with us, and He is not bound by anything but His Word. He loves to hear our heart, but He's not bound by our words—He's bound by His Word. God said, "Put Me in remembrance" (Isaiah 43:26). He didn't say this because He has a bad memory. He likes to be reminded of His Word and have it quoted back to Him. In Jeremiah 1:12, He said, "I am watching over My word to perform it" (NASB). He's not watching over our word to perform it; He is watching over His own Word to perform it.

If you heard me pray, the majority of my prayers consist of "Father, You said . . ." or "Your Word says . . ." Mainly, I remind God of what He promised. His words will move Him more than my words will. That's why each prayer in this book is based entirely on God's Word. I encourage you to pray these prayers out loud so that you release His Word into the atmosphere and get it down into your spirit.

Hebrews 4:12 says, "The word of God is *living* and *active* and *full of power*" (AMP, emphasis added). First, the Word is *living*. "All Scripture is God-breathed" (2 Timothy 3:16 NIV). He breathed the same life-giving breath that created mankind from the dust of the ground into His written Word and infused it with life and supernatural power. You can't say that about any other written words.

Second, God's Word is *active*. It's not passive. It's not neutral. When you pray or speak it over your situation, it *goes to work*. God said, "I am watching over my word to *perform it*" (Jeremiah 1:12 ESV, emphasis added). When you pray His Word, the God of the universe watches over His Word to perform it. And because it is performed by the most powerful force in the universe, it is full of supernatural, wonder-working power.

And let's remember that Jesus Himself is the Word. "In the beginning was the Word, and the Word was with God, and the Word was God. . . . And the Word became flesh and dwelt among us" (John 1:1, 14). God and His Word are one and the same. When we pray or speak His Word out loud, we are releasing God and His power into our situation!

God said, "He who has My word, let him speak My word faithfully. . . . Is not My word like a fire . . . and like a hammer that breaks the rock in pieces?" (Jeremiah 23:28–29). God's Word is so powerful that it's like a fire that burns down and a hammer that breaks through every obstacle in your path. The more you pray His Word, the more you will see it go to work and bring mighty breakthroughs in your life!

Psalm 138:2 says, "You have magnified Your word above all Your name." Why has He magnified His word above His name? Because if He didn't keep His word, His name wouldn't mean much. He called Himself Jehovah Rapha, the God who heals, but if He didn't keep His word to heal, that name wouldn't mean anything. He called Himself Jehovah Jireh, the God who provides, but if He didn't keep His word to provide our needs, that name wouldn't mean anything. Keeping His word is what gives meaning to each of His names, so He magnifies His word above His name.

Scripture says, "No matter how many promises God has made, they are 'Yes' in Christ. And so through him *the 'Amen' is spoken by us*" (2 Corinthians 1:20 NIV, emphasis added). When we pray God's Word, we put our amen—our "so be it" agreement—on His promises. By agreeing with His Word, we give it permission to manifest in our life. *Pray the promises, not the problem.* Often, the way people pray does more harm than good because they just repeat the problem. Praying "complainy" prayers that repeat the problem will keep you stuck where you are. The purpose of prayer is not to give God our list of complaints and tell Him how bad our situation is. He already knows. He has compassion for your situation, but what moves Him to act is *praying His Word back to Him in faith*.

Praying with Faith

The second component of power prayers is *praying with real faith*. The Bible defines faith as "the assurance (the confirmation, the title deed) of the things [we] hope for . . . the conviction of their reality [faith perceiving as real fact what is not revealed to the senses]" (Hebrews 11:1 AMPC). It is believing that we already have the title deed to the things God promised us. They are already reality and fact in the spirit realm; we are just waiting for them to manifest in the natural realm. Jesus said, "Whatever you ask for in prayer, believe that you *have received it* [past tense], and it *will be* yours [future tense]" (Mark 11:24 NIV, emphasis added).

We have to believe that we already have the title deed to the things we are praying for. They already belong to us. If God said it, we believe it; that settles it. It doesn't matter what a doctor or someone else says. It doesn't matter what the natural facts say. It doesn't matter how hopeless it seems. We believe God above all else. We know He's a miracle-working, mountain-moving, Red Sea–parting, promise-keeping God, and nothing is impossible with Him! This is the kind of faith behind power prayers that gets results. Conversely, James 1:6–7 says we can't expect to receive anything from God without faith. "Let him ask [pray] in faith, with no doubting, for he who doubts is like a wave of the sea driven and tossed by the wind. For let not that man suppose that he will receive anything from the Lord."

Faithless religious prayers won't do. God is not impressed by religiosity or flowery eloquence. Begging or complaining prayers won't do either. Faith alone is what moves God. It is the currency of heaven. Praying without faith is like going shopping without money. Jesus said, "Whatever things you ask in prayer, *believing*, you will receive" (Matthew 21:22, emphasis added). The operative word there is *believing*. When we pray, we must truly *believe* that God will do what we are praying for. The prayers in this book are based on God's Word, which satisfies the first key for power prayers, but it's up to you to add your faith to them. Hebrews 4:2 says, "The word which they heard did not profit them, not being mixed with faith in those who heard it." It's the combination of the *Word and faith* that wins the day.

Praying with Persistence

The third component of power prayers is *persistence*. Jesus taught His disciples not one but two parables about the importance of persistence in prayer—the parable of the persistent widow (see Luke 18:1–8) and the parable of the persistent friend (see Luke 11:5–8). He said, "At all times [we] ought to pray and not give up and lose heart" (Luke 18:1 AMP). So many people give up praying and believing right before their breakthrough. They start out strong, but as time goes on and they don't see their situation changing, they slowly give up. Jesus told these parables to encourage us to persevere in prayer and never give up. It's not enough to ask God a few times but then quit. We must be like the persistent widow and the persistent friend and keep praying as long as it takes.

God is not like a drive-thru window where we place our order at the first window and receive it a few minutes later at the second window. He has His own timetable and agenda. The need for persistence is not because God is sitting up in heaven with His arms folded waiting for us to ask Him another thousand times before He acts. No, the persistence is for us. "We also glory in tribulations, knowing that tribulation produces perseverance; and *perseverance, character*; and character, hope" (Romans 5:3–4, emphasis added). Rewind: "And perseverance, *character*." Character is what God is after by making us persevere. He's not cold, uncaring, indifferent, or any of the other lies the enemy or our frustrated thoughts tell us. When He promised to work all things together for our good, this is part of the "good" He meant (see Romans 8:28). He makes us press through adversity and wait for our breakthrough to build our character, spiritual muscles, and a faith that is tough and resilient, as well as to make our roots go deeper in Him. There is no other way for Him to do it. We only develop these things by pressing through adversity and waiting.

The enemy will do everything he can to discourage you from persisting in prayer because he doesn't want you to get your breakthrough and walk in victory. Especially if you've been praying for a while and your prayers haven't produced the results you hoped for, he will tell you, *Your prayers aren't working. God doesn't care about you. If He was going to answer you, He would have done it by now.* But I have found that God often does His best work when we don't see anything happening. He is working in the unseen realm. Faith is in the unseen realm. If we can see it, we don't need faith. Don't ever let the enemy or your own thoughts convince you that your prayers aren't doing any good. Your prayers are powerful, and if you don't give up, your breakthrough will come in God's perfect timing.

The book of Daniel gives us another reason why we must be persistent in prayer. Daniel had been fasting and praying for twenty-one days when suddenly an angel appeared to him.

> "Don't be afraid, Daniel. Since the first day you began to pray for understanding and to humble yourself before your God, your request has been heard in heaven. I have come in answer to your prayer. But for twenty-one days the spirit prince of the kingdom of Persia blocked my way. Then Michael, one of the archangels, came to help me, and I left him there with the spirit prince of the kingdom of Persia."
>
> Daniel 10:12–13 NLT

The angel told Daniel that his prayer had been heard the first day he prayed and that he had been dispatched with the answer to it. But a demonic spirit blocked him from getting to Daniel with the answer to his prayer. The archangel Michael, captain of the angel armies, joined the battle, and the angel finally got through after twenty-one days. This stunning passage peels back the veil and shows that there can be demonic interference to our prayers in the spirit realm. This angel had to do battle with a powerful demonic spirit for twenty-one days and call for backup just to get through with the answer to Daniel's prayer. What if Daniel had given up and stopped praying during those twenty-one days? His answer may not have come. So, be persistent in prayer. Refuse to give up. Show the enemy you are more determined than he is.

If you pray throughout the day about everything and pray the Word with faith and persistence, then I guarantee you will see God move in your life like never before. You will experience levels of His blessings, favor, and victory you never imagined. So, let's go pray some power prayers!

I
RELATIONSHIP WITH GOD

1 Prayer of Salvation

HEAVENLY FATHER, Your Word says, "All have sinned and fall short of the glory of God." It says the penalty of sin is spiritual death and eternal separation from You, but You gave us the free gift of salvation in Jesus Christ. "Salvation is found in no one else, for there is no other name under heaven given to mankind by which we must be saved." Father, I confess that I am a sinner in need of salvation that is only found in Jesus Christ.

You said, "If you declare with your mouth, 'Jesus is Lord,' and believe in your heart that God raised him from the dead, you will be saved." I declare out loud that Jesus Christ is Lord. I believe in my heart that He died for my sins and that You raised Him from the dead. Lord Jesus, I ask You to come into my heart and be my Lord and Savior. I surrender my life to You. I repent of all my sins and ask You to forgive me and cleanse me of all unrighteousness by Your precious blood. Thank You that You took all my sins upon You at the cross and gave me Your perfect righteousness. Because of Your finished work on the cross, I am blameless before God and have boldness to enter His presence without any guilt, shame, or condemnation.

Father, You said, "If anyone is in Christ, he is a new creation; old things have passed away; behold, all things have become new." I ask You to make me that new creation in Christ. Mold and shape me into the person You created me to be. Fill me with Your Holy Spirit, guide me in Your truth, and help me walk in Your ways. Help me to shine the light of Christ and be a great witness for Him everywhere I go. Thank You for the gift of my eternal salvation in Christ and the wonderful things You have in store for my future. I pray all these things in the precious name of Jesus, Amen.

SCRIPTURE REFERENCES

Romans 3:23
Romans 6:23
Acts 4:12 NIV
Romans 10:9 NIV
1 John 1:9
2 Corinthians 5:21
Hebrews 10:19
Romans 8:1
2 Corinthians 5:17

2 Prayer of Rededication

HEAVENLY FATHER, I confess that I have sinned and wandered from You. I ask You to forgive me, cleanse me of all unrighteousness, and put me back on the path of Your will for my life. Jesus, I confess that You are my Lord and Savior, and I rededicate my life wholly to You. I commit to serving You the rest of my days and doing my best to glorify You with my life.

Father, I'm reminded of the parable of the prodigal son Jesus told. After the son went away from the father and engaged in a life of sin and rebellion, one day "he came to himself" and returned to his father. The father saw him afar off and ran to him. He didn't scold or condemn him. He embraced him and put the best robe and a ring on him. Then he had a party to celebrate his son's return. Father, thank You that You are that Father. You never gave up on me or stopped loving me. You have been so patient. Thank You for welcoming me back with open arms.

Father, help me to never stray again but to live the rest of my life serving You and becoming the person You created me to be. I ask You to restore the years the locusts and cankerworms destroyed through my sin and independence from You. Help me to redeem my time left on earth and make a difference in this world for Your Kingdom and Your glory. I pray this in the precious name of Jesus, Amen.

SCRIPTURE REFERENCES

Luke 15:11–24   Joel 2:25

3 Prayer to Receive God's Love

HEAVENLY FATHER, Your Word says, "Look with wonder at the depth of the Father's marvelous love that he has lavished on us! He has called us and made us his very own beloved children" (1 John 3:1 TPT). You loved me when I was a sinner and away from You. You loved me before I ever loved or served You. You love me because I am Your creation and child. Help me truly receive Your love to the depths of my soul and spirit. Let it wash over and permeate every fiber of my being.

Lord, I'm reminded of how the Apostle John referred to himself as "the disciple whom Jesus loved" five times in his Gospel. He didn't boast about his love for You; he boasted about Your love for him. He dwelled on Your love for him and reminded himself of it often. I pray that I would do the same. Let me soak in Your love, meditate on it, and receive it daily.

Correct any skewed perception I have of You. Help me to know that You love me because I am Your child. You said about Jesus, "This is My beloved Son, in whom I am well pleased" (Matthew 3:17) before He preached a message, performed a single miracle, or did anything for Your Kingdom. I am Your beloved child in whom You are well pleased. I am unconditionally loved by You. Your Word says nothing I have ever done or will do could make You love me any less.

[If you had a negative experience with your earthly father:] Father, help me understand that You are not like my earthly father. You will never harm, abandon, reject, or neglect me. Heal my soul from any wound or perception from my upbringing that hinders me from receiving Your love, acceptance, and approval. Help me forgive my father and anyone else who tainted my view of You.

Father, whatever wounded me and made it harder to receive Your love, I ask You to heal it completely. If I have walls around my heart, I ask You to melt them. Make my heart tender and open to You. Fill me with Your love, so I can love myself and others the way You want me to. I pray all these things in the name of Jesus, Amen.

SCRIPTURES REFERENCES

1 John 3:1 TPT	John 3:16	Ephesians 3:19 NLT
Romans 5:8	John 13:23, 19:26,	Romans 8:38 NLT
1 John 4:10	20:2, 21:7, 21:20	

4 Prayer of Repentance

HEAVENLY FATHER, I humble myself before You and repent for all the ways I have sinned against You in thought, word, deed, and attitudes of the heart. Thank You that Your Word says, "If we confess our sins, [You are] faithful and just to forgive us our sins and to cleanse us from all unrighteousness." Proverbs says, "He who covers his sins will not prosper, but whoever confesses and forsakes them will have mercy." Father, I don't want to cover anything. I know You see all things and nothing is hidden from Your sight. So, I confess [name anything specific you need to confess]. I ask You to forgive me for falling short of Your standard and sinning against You. Cleanse me of all unrighteousness by the blood of Jesus and close every door to the enemy.

Lord, I understand that the word *repent* is more than confessing or saying I am sorry—it is turning away from my sins. It is rejecting and refusing to engage in old sin patterns. It is a true change of heart toward those sins and a determination to leave them behind. Lord, You said, "Without Me you can do nothing," so I ask You to help me truly repent. By the power of Your Holy Spirit, set me free from repeating the same sins. Deliver me from every sin pattern, stronghold, bondage, generational curse, and work of darkness in my life. You said it is for freedom Jesus set me free, and whom the Son sets free is free indeed. Help me to walk in the liberty for which Christ Jesus set me free.

Lord, Your Word says, "Be holy, for I am holy." Hebrews says, "Pursue peace with all people, and holiness, without which no one will see the Lord." You never tell us to do anything without giving us the ability to do it, so thank You for empowering me to walk in holiness, resist temptation, and live a life that honors You. I pray all these things in the mighty name of Jesus, Amen.

SCRIPTURE REFERENCES

1 John 1:9	Galatians 5:1	Hebrews 12:14
Proverbs 28:13	John 8:36	
John 15:5	1 Peter 1:16	

5 Prayer of Surrender

HEAVENLY FATHER, I come before You with a heart of humility and surrender. You are the God of the universe. You have all wisdom, knowledge, and power. You know the plans You have for me, "plans to prosper [me] and not to harm [me], plans to give [me] hope and a future." You have the best plan for my life, and nothing I could conceive could top Your plans. So, I make a decision right now to surrender my spirit, mind, will, emotions, decisions, relationships, finances, career/assignment, and everything in my life to You. I repent for all the times I haven't been surrendered to You. I ask You to set me free from any pride, self-sufficiency, independence, rebellion, wrong beliefs, or anything else that has hindered me from living a life of total surrender to You.

Father, help me to live by the words of Jesus, who said, "Not my will, but yours be done." May Your will be done in my life as it is in heaven. Your Word says, "You are not your own; you were bought at a price." Remind me that I was purchased for the highest price—the precious blood of the Lamb—and that my life is not my own. Help me to live with a yielded spirit and give You a fresh surrender every day so that I can become all You created me to be and fulfill every plan You have for my life.

Your Word says, "Trust in the LORD with all your heart and lean not on your own understanding; in all your ways submit to him, and he will make your paths straight." Help me to trust You completely, even when I can't discern or don't understand Your plan. Help me to live by this verse and submit all my ways to You, knowing that the safest and most blessed place to be is in Your perfect will. It's in the name above all names, my Lord and Savior Jesus Christ, that I pray all these things, Amen.

SCRIPTURE REFERENCES

Jeremiah 29:11 NIV
Luke 22:42 NIV
1 Corinthians 6:19–20 NIV
Proverbs 3:5–6 NIV

6 Prayer to Put God First

HEAVENLY FATHER, I humble myself before You and worship You as the God of the universe. You created me and brought me into this world. It's Your breath in my lungs. I wouldn't have woken up this morning if it had not been for You. I wouldn't have my salvation or anything good in my life without You. "Every good gift and every perfect gift is from above." "In [You] we live and move and have our being." "In [You] all things hold together." You deserve to be first place in my life. No person, pursuit, or desire should come close to You. Help me to keep You first place in my heart and in my daily decisions, relationships, finances, career, and every area of my life. Help me to live by the first and greatest commandment: "You shall love the Lord your God with all your heart, with all your soul, and with all your strength." Help me not to have any idols before You.

Matthew says, "Seek the Kingdom of God above all else, and live righteously, and he will give you everything you need." I pray that I would seek You and Your Kingdom above all else. Help me to start each day putting You first—setting aside focused time to pray, study Your Word, worship, and listen to You. Help me to honor You with the firstfruits of my finances. Your Word says, "Glorify God with all your wealth, honoring him with your firstfruits, with every increase that comes to you. Then every dimension of your life will overflow with blessings." As I am obedient to tithe the first tenth of my income, which the Bible says belongs to You and is holy, I will enjoy an overflow of Your blessings.

Lord Jesus, You told one of the churches in Revelation that they had done good deeds, resisted evil, and persevered through hardship, but You said, "Nevertheless I have this against you, that you have left your first love." I repent if I have ever left my first love, and I pray I would always keep You as my first love. I love You. I thank You. I praise, magnify, and honor You. You are worthy to be number one in my heart and life! It's in Jesus' precious name I pray, Amen.

SCRIPTURE REFERENCES

James 1:17
Acts 17:28 NIV
Colossians 1:17 NIV
Deuteronomy 6:5; Mark 12:30
Matthew 6:33 NLT
Proverbs 3:9-10 TPT
Leviticus 27:30
Revelation 2:2-4

7 Prayer to Abide in Christ

LORD JESUS, You said in John 15, "Abide in Me, and I in you. . . . I am the vine, you are the branches. . . . Without Me you can do nothing. . . . If you abide in Me, and My words abide in you, you will ask what you desire, and it shall be done for you." You used the word *abide* seven times in this passage, more than a word was repeated in any other passage in the Bible. Help me to understand how important abiding in You is. That word means to remain in continuous fellowship and communication with You—not just on Sunday mornings or during my morning "quiet time," but throughout the day. You said that when I do this, I can ask whatever I desire, and it will be done for me. What an amazing offer!

Help me to abide in You every day, starting with my devotional time in the morning where I seek You first, study Your Word, pray, offer thanksgiving and praise, and quietly listen to Your still, small voice. Then, help me not to barrel through my day and forget about You in the busyness of life, but to make my relationship with You an integral part of my day and every facet of my life. Help me to make a habit of dialoguing with You throughout the day and listening to Your Holy Spirit's guidance. Make me one who successfully abides in You to the point that I exude Your light, love, and character in everything I do. I pray all these things in the name of Jesus, Amen.

SCRIPTURE REFERENCES
John 15:4-5, 7

8 Prayer for Deeper Walk with God

HEAVENLY FATHER, I have a desire to know You more and have a deeper relationship with You. In Ezekiel 47, You gave the prophet Ezekiel a vision of water flowing from the temple—some ankle deep, some knee deep, some waist deep, and some so deep that a person had to swim. Lord, help me not to be content staying in ankle-, knee-, or waist-deep water but to press into the deep with You. I want more than a superficial, shallow relationship with You Your Word says, "Deep calls unto deep."

Father, I am reminded that Your temple had three sections—the outer court, the Most Holy Place, and the innermost part, the Holy of Holies, where Your presence dwelled. I don't want to live in the outer court, but I desire to press into the Holy of Holies, experience Your presence, and have an intimate relationship with You. Your Word says, "Let your roots grow down into him, and let your lives be built on him." Lord, let my roots grow deep in You, and let my life be built on You. Help me to go deeper with You every day as I pursue You in prayer, study Your Word, give You praise and worship, and involve You intimately in every area of my life. I pray all these things in Jesus' holy name, Amen.

SCRIPTURE REFERENCES
Ezekiel 47   Psalm 42:7   Colossians 2:7 NLT

9 Prayer to be Holy

HEAVENLY FATHER, You are a holy God. The angels around Your throne cry out day and night saying, "Holy, holy, holy, Lord God Almighty." You commanded us to be holy, saying, "Be holy, for I am holy." Your Word says, "Work at living a holy life, for those who are not holy will not see the Lord." I pray that I would be holy and pursue holiness. Help me to be:

- Holy in my thoughts. Put a guard around my mind. Help me to have the mind of Christ and think pure, godly thoughts. Your Word says, "Fix your thoughts on what is true, and honorable, and right, and pure, and lovely, and admirable."
- Holy in my heart—my desires, attitudes, motives, emotions. "Create in me a clean heart, O God, and renew a steadfast spirit within me." You said, "Above all else, guard your heart, for everything you do flows from it."
- Holy in my words. Help me to remember the power of my words and only speak words that are godly, edifying, positive, and faith-filled. "Do not let unwholesome [foul, profane, worthless, vulgar] words ever come out of your mouth, but only such speech as is good for building up others, according to the need and the occasion, so that it will be a blessing to those who hear [you speak]." Jesus said, "But I tell you, on the day of judgment people will have to give an accounting for every careless or useless word they speak."
- Holy in my body. Help me to keep my body, which is the temple of the Holy Spirit, pure and holy, and not defile it through sexual immorality, substance abuse, or other means. Your Word says, "Present your bodies a living sacrifice, holy, acceptable to God, which is your reasonable service. And do not be conformed to this world."

Father, help me to resist temptation in all these areas and not take the bait of Satan. As Jesus taught us to pray in the Lord's Prayer, "Do not lead [me] into temptation, but deliver [me] from the evil one." Your Word says, "God is faithful, and he will not let you be tempted beyond your ability, but with the temptation he will also provide the way of escape." When I am tempted in any of these areas, help me to take the way of escape You provide and not enter into sin. Thank You that I don't have to resist temptation and be holy in my own strength and ability. The Helper, the Holy Spirit, lives on the inside of me and helps me live the Christian life. Thank You for helping me "walk worthy of the Lord, fully pleasing [You]." I pray all these things in Jesus' holy name, Amen.

SCRIPTURE REFERENCES

Revelation 4:8	Psalm 51:10	Romans 12:1–2
1 Peter 1:16	Proverbs 4:23 NIV	Matthew 6:13
Hebrews 12:14 NLT	Ephesians 4:29 AMP	1 Corinthians 10:13 ESV
Philippians 4:8 NLT	Matthew 12:36 AMP	Colossians 1:10

10 Prayer to be More Christlike

HEAVENLY FATHER, You desire every believer to be conformed to the image of Christ. Your Word says the Holy Spirit gradually transforms us from glory to glory into the image of Christ. Help me to be a willing and yielded participant in this transformation process. Mold me and shape me and help me to become more like Jesus every day.

As the apostle Paul wrote, I pray that I would be crucified with Christ and that it would no longer be me who lives, but Christ who lives within me. I pray as John the Baptist said that I would decrease and let Jesus increase in me. Help me to crucify my flesh daily so that people see more of Jesus and less of me.

In Psalm 17:15, David wrote, "I shall be satisfied when I awake in Your likeness." I pray that I would awaken in the likeness of Christ more and more each day. Give me the mind, heart, and character of Christ. Help me to love others with His love. Help me to be His fragrant aroma everywhere I go. Like the moon reflects the light of the sun, help me reflect the light of Christ. I pray all these things in the precious name of Jesus, Amen.

SCRIPTURE REFERENCES

Romans 8:29	John 3:30	Galatians 2:20
2 Corinthians 3:18	2 Corinthians 2:14-16	Psalm 17:15

11 Prayer to Walk in the Holy Spirit

HEAVENLY FATHER, thank You for Your Holy Spirit who lives inside of me—the wisest and most powerful force in the universe, the same Spirit who raised Jesus from the dead and anointed Him to do miracles. The Spirit of wisdom, counsel, knowledge, and understanding. My helper, comforter, strengthener, counselor, advocate, intercessor, and standby. Thank You that I don't have to live the Christian life in my own strength and ability, but the Greater One is there to help me in every way. Your Word tells us to walk in the Spirit and not the flesh and to sow into the Spirit and not the flesh. Help me to die to my flesh daily and be continually filled with the Holy Spirit.

I pray that the Holy Spirit's fruit—love, joy, peace, patience, kindness, goodness, faithfulness, gentleness, and self-control—would be evident in my life so that I can represent Jesus well everywhere I go. Even when things don't go my way and I am pressed by challenges, I pray that I would display the fruit of the Spirit instead of my flesh.

Your Word says, "Walk and live [habitually] in the [Holy] Spirit [responsive to and controlled and guided by the Spirit]." Help me to be sensitive to the leadings and promptings of the Holy Spirit so that I can navigate people and life with divine wisdom. You said, "As many as are led by the Spirit of God, these are sons of God." Help me to be led by the Holy Spirit in every decision I make and every interaction I have with people.

Lord, You said, "You shall receive power when the Holy Spirit has come upon you; and you shall be witnesses to Me in Jerusalem, and in all Judea and Samaria, and to the end of the earth." You said we would do the same works You did, and supernatural signs would follow us by the power of the Holy Spirit. Help me to walk in the power of the Holy Spirit so I can minister healing to the sick and do other miraculous works that lead people to Christ and glorify You. I pray all these things in the mighty name of Jesus, Amen.

SCRIPTURE REFERENCES

Romans 8:11	Galatians 6:8	Romans 8:14
Isaiah 11:2	Galatians 5:22	Acts 1:8
John 14:16	Galatians 5:16 AMPC	

12 Prayer to Hear the Voice of God

LORD JESUS, when You visited Martha and Mary's home, Martha was busy and distracted, but Mary was sitting at Your feet listening to every word You said. When Martha complained and wanted Mary to help her serve, You said, "Martha, Martha, you are worried and troubled about many things. But one thing is needed, and Mary has chosen that good part." You said *one thing is needed*—not two, not three, not five. *One*. And that one thing was Mary listening to Your words. You said, "Everyone then who *hears* these words of mine and *does them* will be like a wise man who built his house on the rock." You said, "Man shall not live by bread alone, but by every word that proceeds from the mouth of God." You want us to *live* by the words You speak to us. So, help me do the one thing that's needed—to spend time listening to You. Help me to be the wise person who hears and does Your words and builds my life upon the Rock. Help me live by every word that proceeds from Your mouth.

Father, Your Word says that You didn't speak to Elijah in wind, earthquake, or fire, but in a *still, small voice*. You don't speak to us in a loud, harsh, or harried voice, but a still, small voice. You're not going to compete with my busyness, distractions, or the noise of the world. So, help me to set aside time every day where I am still, quiet, and focused on hearing Your voice. Thank You that when I seek to hear You, You promise to instruct me and teach me in the way I should go and counsel me with Your loving eye upon me. Thank You that, as I listen and obey what You tell me, I will make great decisions and experience more of Your blessings and favor in my life. I pray all these things in the precious name of Jesus, Amen.

SCRIPTURE REFERENCES

Luke 10:38–42
Matthew 7:24 ESV, emphasis added
Matthew 4:4
1 Kings 19:12
Psalm 32:8

13 Prayer of Thanksgiving

Heavenly Father, I come to You with a heart brimming with thanksgiving. I want to be like the leper who returned and give You thanks for everything You have done in my life. Thank You for the breath in my lungs. Thank You that I woke up this morning and had strength to get out of bed. Thank You for my eternal salvation. Thank You for my freedom. Thank You for the roof over my head, the food on my table, and clean water to drink when billions of people in the world don't have these things. Thank You for my health. Thank You for my family [mention your spouse and children, if applicable], friends, and everyone You have put in my life. Thank You for my church and pastors. Thank You for my job [or business or retirement]. Thank You for opening the right doors and closing the wrong doors. Thank You for every good break. "Blessed be the Lord, who daily loads us with benefits." Thank You for daily loading me with benefits.

Thank You for Your unfailing, unconditional love. Thank You for loving me when I was still a sinner and before I ever loved You. Thank You for Your goodness, mercy, grace, forgiveness, faithfulness, protection, provision, guidance, and favor all the days of my life.

Father, help me to zoom out and realize how blessed I am. Billions of people would trade places with me in a heartbeat. Help me to live with a spirit of gratitude and be thankful for every blessing. Your Word says to "give thanks in all circumstances; for this is God's will for you in Christ Jesus." If I had a thousand tongues, it wouldn't be enough to thank You for all that You've done for me! I pray this in Jesus' precious name, Amen.

SCRIPTURE REFERENCES

Psalm 100:4
Luke 17:12–19
Psalm 68:19
1 Thessalonians 5:18 NIV
James 1:17

14 Prayer of Praise

HEAVENLY FATHER, I praise You because You are holy and perfect in all Your ways. You are worthy of all praise, glory, and honor.

I praise You because You are love. You loved me while I was yet a sinner and before I ever loved You. You love me with unconditional, unlimited love. You have loved me so well.

I praise You because You sent Jesus to die on the cross and save me when I couldn't save myself. You're the God who saves, delivers, sets free, and heals.

I praise You because You are good all the time, regardless of my circumstances.

I praise You because You are Elohim, the Creator and Sustainer of Life. All things have been created through You and for You. You were before all things, and You hold everything together.

I praise You because You are the great I AM. Everything I need is found in You.

You are El Shaddai, God Almighty, the All-Sufficient One. You're an awesome, mighty God.

You are El Elyon, the Most High God. You're the God who sits on the throne. You have all power and authority. Mountains melt like wax in Your presence.

I praise You because You are Jehovah Baal Perazim, the God of the breakthrough. You are breaking through my enemies and every obstacle in my path like the breakthrough of many waters.

I praise You because You are Jehovah Rapha, the God who heals me. You heal not only my body but also my soul.

You are Jehovah Jireh, the Lord my provider. You are my Shepherd, I shall not lack.

You are my protecter and deliverer; my rock, refuge, and fortress; my shield and buckler; my strong tower from the enemy. You cover me under Your wings and surround me with mighty angels.

You are Jehovah Sabaoth, the Lord of Hosts, who commands the angel armies.

You are Jehovah Shammah, the God who is with me wherever I go.

You are Jehovah Shalom, my peace.

You are El Roi, the God who sees everything. A sparrow doesn't fall to the ground without You knowing.

You are worthy of all praise, glory, and honor! Let Your praises be continually in my mouth. In Jesus' name I pray, Amen.

SCRIPTURE REFERENCES

Psalm 22:3	Genesis 17:1	Exodus 15:26
Romans 5:8	Psalm 78:35	Genesis 22:13–14
Colossians 1:16–17	Psalm 97:5	Psalm 23:1
Exodus 3:14	2 Samuel 5:20	Psalm 91

15 Prayer to Trust God More

HEAVENLY FATHER, thank You that You are a faithful, all-wise, all-knowing, loving Father and worthy of my complete trust. You've never let me down, and You never will. Your Word says, "Trust in the Lord with all your heart, and lean not on your own understanding." Help me to trust You more in every area of my life and every situation I encounter and not lean on my own understanding. Help me to rest in the promise of Jeremiah 29:11—that You know the plans You have for me, plans to prosper me and not to harm me, plans to give me a hope and a future. You have the best plans for my life.

Father, help me to trust You even when I don't know or understand Your plans. Your ways are not my ways, and Your thoughts are not my thoughts, but as high as the heavens are above the earth, so are Your ways and thoughts higher than mine. So, help me let go of the need to know why, the need to understand everything, and the need to know how, when, and with whom everything is going to happen. David said, "My times are in Your hand." Help me to trust Your timing and not get impatient. When I'm facing a challenge, help me to do my part but trust You with the outcome. When I walk through a dark valley and I can't see the way out, help me to trust that You are with me and will make a way where there seems to be no way and bring me out with the victory. You're the fourth Man in the fire. When I face unfair situations, help me to trust that You are my defender, You are working all things together for my good, and You will pay me back for every unfair situation.

Father, Your Word tells us almost one hundred times to trust in You and promises abundant blessings for doing so. Psalm 2:12 says that I am blessed when I trust You. Isaiah 26:3 says that I will have perfect peace when I keep my mind stayed on You because I trust in You. Psalm 18:30 says that You are a shield to me when I trust in You. Psalm 32:10 says that mercy will surround me when I trust You. Psalm 31:19 says that Your goodness is great toward me when I trust You. Psalm 28:7 says that You help me when I trust You. So, I pray that I would trust You in a deep, unshakable, and consistent way in every area of my life. I ask all these things in the most trustworthy name of all, my Lord and Savior Jesus Christ, Amen.

SCRIPTURE REFERENCES

Proverbs 3:5–6	Psalm 2:12	Psalm 31:19
Jeremiah 29:11	Isaiah 26:3	Psalm 28:7
Isaiah 55:8–9	Psalm 18:30	
Psalm 31:15	Psalm 32:10	

16 Prayer for More Faith

HEAVENLY FATHER, You created the whole universe with the words of Your mouth, parted the Red Sea, and raised Jesus from the dead after three days. You are the great I AM, and nothing is too hard for You. You are a miracle-working, mountain-moving, way-making, promise-keeping God. Help me to have big faith because You are a great, big God, and absolutely nothing is impossible with You. Jesus said, "If you can believe, all things are possible to him who believes." He put it back on us to believe. He also said, "Whatever things you ask when you pray, believe that you receive them, and you will have them." Help me not to try to figure it out or overthink. Help me not to limit You through limiting thoughts, doubts, reasonings, or excuses but to simply believe You with childlike faith. Help me to have the mindset that *if You said it, I believe it*. I pray that I would believe You over what I see, the natural facts, what the doctor or someone else said, what the enemy whispered in my ear, or my own thoughts and emotions.

When I am feeling weak in faith, I ask You to revive, refresh, and strengthen my faith. Help me to have tough, resilient, unshakable faith. Guard my heart and mind from fear, worry, doubt, lies, and anything else that would undermine my faith. Help me to take steps every day to feed my faith by studying Your Word, listening to faith-inspiring messages, and being around faith-filled people. Thank You that, as my faith grows, I will see more of Your promises manifested in my life. I pray all these things in the powerful name of Jesus, Amen.

SCRIPTURE REFERENCES

James 1:6–7	Hebrews 11:6	Mark 9:23
Hebrews 10:38	Romans 14:23	Mark 11:24

17 Prayer for Obedience

HEAVENLY FATHER, I humble myself before You and acknowledge that You are far wiser than me, know all things, and have the best plan for my life. When You tell me to do or not do something in Your Word or by Your Spirit, it's not because You are trying to control me but because You want the best for me. Your Word says, "If you are willing and obedient, you shall eat the good of the land." Help me to be willing and obedient so that I can eat the good of the land and experience Your blessings and favor. Help me to trust and obey You, even when what You tell me doesn't make sense to my natural mind or is not something I want to do in my flesh. I pray that I would live surrendered to You and have the mindset of Christ: not my will but Yours be done.

Your Word says, "Don't just listen to God's word. You must do what it says. Otherwise, you are only fooling yourselves. . . . And if you do what it says and don't forget what you heard, then God will bless you for doing it." Lord, when I read Your Word or go to church and hear my pastor preach the Word, help me to actually *do* what the Word says consistently. Help me also to be sensitive and obedient to Your still, small voice and the gentle promptings of Your Holy Spirit. You said, "If you faithfully obey the voice of the LORD your God, being careful to do all his commandments . . . all these blessings shall come upon you and overtake you." Thank You that as I seek to obey You in all things, Your blessings will chase me and overtake me! I pray all these things in the precious name of Jesus, Amen.

SCRIPTURE REFERENCES

John 14:15
Luke 6:46
Isaiah 1:19

Proverbs 3:5
James 1:22–25 NLT
Romans 8:14

Deuteronomy 28:1–2 ESV

18 Prayer for Fresh Fire

Lord Jesus, You said, "I know your works, that you are neither cold nor hot. I could wish you were cold or hot. So then, because you are lukewarm, and neither cold nor hot, I will vomit you out of My mouth." Help me not to be a lukewarm, casual Christian that You want to vomit out of Your mouth. Help me not to allow the cares of this world, the trials of life, or people to dampen my flame. Help me to stay white-hot for You.

Your Word tells us to "stir up (rekindle the embers of, fan the flame of, and keep burning) the [gracious] gift of God, [the inner fire] that is in you." Help me to stir up the inner fire within me and never let it die down to a faint ember. Hebrews 12:29 says that You are an all-consuming fire. Consume me with Your holy fire, and burn up everything in me that is not of You. All four gospels say that You will baptize me with the Holy Spirit and fire. I ask You to fill me with Your Holy Spirit and fire. Give me fresh fire, fresh wind, fresh vision, fresh anointing, fresh power, and fresh revelation, in the mighty name of Jesus. I thank You for it and receive it by faith, in Jesus' name, Amen.

SCRIPTURE REFERENCES

Revelation 3:15–16   2 Timothy 1:6 AMPC   Hebrews 12:29

II
RELATIONSHIP WITH OTHERS

19 Prayer to Walk in Love

HEAVENLY FATHER, Your Word is clear that love is the most important thing to You. The two greatest commandments are to love You with all our heart, soul, and mind, and to love others like we love ourselves. Your Word says, "Above all things have intense and unfailing love for one another," and "Above all these things put on love, which is the bond of perfection." It says, "Your love for one another will prove to the world that you are my disciples." Not by how well we know the Bible. Not by how often we go to church. Not by our social media posts about You. People will know we are Your disciples by our love walk.

So, Father, help me to improve my love walk. Help me to love everyone—even people who are very different from me and with whom I may not agree and people who may rub my flesh the wrong way. Help me to rise above my flesh and love with Your supernatural *agape* love. Your love is patient, kind, does not envy, does not boast, is not proud, does not dishonor others, is not selfish, is not easily angered, and keeps no record of wrongs. It bears all things, believes all things, hopes all things, endures all things, and never fails.

Lord, You said, "Love your enemies, bless those who curse you, do good to those who hate you, and pray for those who spitefully use you and persecute you. . . . For if you love those who love you, what reward have you? Do not even the tax collectors do the same?" Help me not just to love those who love me and are good to me but to love even my enemies. Heal my soul from the pain people have caused, and help me to love as if I've never been hurt. I pray all these things in the matchless name of Jesus, Amen.

SCRIPTURE REFERENCES

Matthew 22:37-40
1 Peter 4:8 AMPC
Colossians 3:14

John 13:35 NLT
1 John 4:8
Matthew 5:44-46

1 Corinthians 13:1-8

---

20 Prayer for Friendship, Community

HEAVENLY FATHER, one of the first things You said after creating Adam was, "It is not good that man should be alone." You created us for relationship. You meant for us to be in community with others. Your Word says, "Two are better than one, because they have a good reward for their labor. For if they fall, one will lift up his companion." Jesus sent His disciples out two by two. You told us not to forsake the gathering of ourselves together. The importance of fellowship and community is stressed throughout Your Word. So, I ask You for more quality friends, fellowship, and community in my life.

Help me to find my tribe, my community. People who understand me and I understand. Friends who are godly eagles, loyal, who share my values, who support and cheer me on, and I do the same for them. Friends who can sharpen me and help me become all You created me to be and reach my destiny. Bless me with the very best friends that I can share life with. You said, "A friend loves at all times, and a brother is born for adversity." I ask for friends who will love me no matter what and stick with me through any adversity. Bring the right people into my life and keep the wrong people out. Give me Holy Spirit wisdom and discernment to choose the best people to surround myself with. You said, "Walk with the wise and become wise, for a companion of fools suffers harm," so help me to associate with wise people and avoid fools.

Your Word says, "Whatever a man sows, that he will also reap." Help me to be proactive, put myself out there, and sow seeds of friendship and community, so that I can reap friendship and community. Help me to invest the time and effort it takes to connect with people socially and spiritually, and not just at work. Deliver me from any walls I have put up with people, and help me to be real and accessible to people. As I do my part, I trust that You will cause me to have rich, meaningful, fulfilling friendships and community. I receive it by faith with thanksgiving, and it's in Jesus' mighty name I pray, Amen.

SCRIPTURE REFERENCES

Genesis 2:18
Ecclesiastes 4:9–10
Mark 6:7

Proverbs 17:17
Hebrews 10:25
Proverbs 13:20 NIV

Galatians 6:7

---

21 Prayer for Single Person Desiring a Mate

HEAVENLY FATHER, You said, "It is not good that man should be alone." You created marriage as the most sacred human relationship, where a man and woman can enjoy their lives together, have a family, and help each other and their children fulfill their

Kingdom destinies. Father, I desire a godly mate with whom I can share my life. You said, "Those who seek the Lord shall not lack any good thing." A godly mate is a good thing. You said, "Ask, and it will be given to you." So, I ask for the best possible mate for me to marry. The person You ordained for me to marry before the foundation of the world. My soul mate. A godly eagle and a person of great character and destiny. Someone who will love and cherish me with his or her whole heart and be faithful to me for life. Someone that I can serve You with, have children with, recreate, travel, and laugh with. Someone with whom I can have the most wonderful life and family.

Father, I ask for great discernment and a healthy picker so that I am attracted to the right kind of person. Keep anyone away from me who would cause pain and destruction in my life. Help me not to get impatient and settle for someone who is less than Your best for me. Help me and my future mate to stay pure as we wait for each other. Get us ready for each other. Deliver us from any pride, selfishness, unhealthiness in our souls, generational curses, strongholds, and bad habits or anything else that would be a stumbling block in our relationship. Do whatever work You need to do in us so that when we meet, we are both saved and fully surrendered to You, have healthy souls, and are able to be the best version of ourselves for each other. I pray that in Your perfect timing You would intersect our paths, and we would have the most amazing Kingdom marriage that glorifies You and lasts a lifetime. I pray all these things in the wonderful name of Jesus, Amen.

SCRIPTURE REFERENCES

Genesis 2:18 Matthew 7:7
Psalm 34:10 Romans 8:32

22 Prayer for Wisdom, Discernment with People

HEAVENLY FATHER, I come to You asking for supernatural wisdom and discernment with people. James 1:5 says, "If any of you lacks wisdom, let him ask of God, who gives to all liberally and without reproach, and it will be given to him." I ask for wisdom to know who to associate with, who to trust, and how to navigate my daily interactions with people. Thank You that Your Spirit, who lives inside of me, is the Spirit of wisdom and counsel and that I always have access to His wisdom. Help me to seek and apply the Holy Spirit's wisdom and counsel in my dealings with people.

Father, You said, "If you want to grow in wisdom, spend time with the wise. Walk with the wicked and you'll eventually become just like them." You said, "Do not be unequally yoked together with unbelievers." Help me to choose wise and godly friends and associates. [If single] Help me to date the right people and only marry the person You have ordained for me to marry. I pray I would never compromise my standards because of loneliness or insecurity, but I would surround myself with the best people who can help me reach my full potential.

Your Word says that the Spirit of truth will guide me in all truth. I ask the Holy Spirit to guide me in truth in my dealings with people. Give me great spiritual discernment and eyes to see past people's facades and words to be able to know their true character and intentions. First John 4:1 says, "Beloved, do not believe every spirit, but test the spirits, whether they are of God." Help me to discern people's spirits so that the enemy cannot use people to deceive, manipulate, or take advantage of me. When I have a check in my spirit about someone, help me not to ignore it or explain it away, but to receive the Holy Spirit's warning. Help me to be careful about who I listen to, allow to influence me, and associate with. Thank You for giving me the wisdom and discernment to choose the right people in my life and to navigate my daily interactions with people the best way. I pray all these things in Jesus' name, Amen.

SCRIPTURE REFERENCES

James 1:5
Proverbs 13:20 TPT
2 Corinthians 6:14
John 16:13
1 John 4:1

23 Prayer for Favor with People

HEAVENLY FATHER, thank You that Psalm 5:12 says that Your favor surrounds me like a shield. Psalm 103:4 says that You have crowned me with favor. I ask for divine favor with everyone with whom I come into contact. Your Word says, "Jesus increased in wisdom and stature, and in favor with God and man." I pray that I would grow in favor with You and people. I ask for the right people to be attracted to me, like me, and go out of their way to be good to me and show me special favor. Bring the right people into my life and keep the wrong people out. Intersect my path with people who have a key to my destiny. Give me great interpersonal skills to relate, interact, and communicate well with people. I pray that everywhere I go, I would experience Your uncommon favor, supernatural doors opening, and Your blessings chasing and overtaking me. In Jesus' precious name I pray, Amen.

SCRIPTURE REFERENCES

Psalm 5:12
Psalm 103:4
Luke 2:52

24 Prayer to Avoid or Resolve Conflict

HEAVENLY FATHER, Your Word says, "When a man's ways please the Lord, He makes even his enemies to be at peace with him." I pray that my ways would please You and that You would cause everyone to be at peace with me. You said, "Do all that you can to live in peace with everyone," and "Pursue peace with all people, and holiness, without which no one will see the Lord." Help me to do everything I can to live in peace and avoid conflict with others. Help me to obey the second greatest commandment—to love others like I love myself—and walk in Christlike love, which is patient, kind, not easily angered, does not keep a record of wrongs, bears all things, and never fails. I pray that I would set the example with those around me. As I do my part, I ask for Your divine peace on every relationship in my life.

Lord, thank You that You have given me authority over all the power of the enemy. You said whatever I bind on earth will be bound in heaven and whatever I loose on earth will be loosed in heaven. So, I bind, rebuke, cut off, and cast out every spirit of strife, division, contention, offense, unforgiveness, and every demonic spirit and work of darkness from my relationships, in Jesus' name. I cover every one of my relationships with the blood of Jesus Christ. I speak peace, harmony, and unity over my relationships, in Jesus' name.

Lord, when conflict occurs, help me to be quick and adept at resolving it. Give me wisdom to navigate conflict in a way that brings reconciliation, unity, and peace. If I need to, help me to humble myself and apologize. Help me and whoever I have conflict with [name anyone you have conflict with] to listen to each other, try to understand each other, and resolve our differences in a way that not only preserves but strengthens our relationship. Your Word says the heart of a king is in Your hands, and like a river, You turn it whichever way You wish. If You can turn a king's heart, You can turn anyone's heart. So, I ask You to turn the other person's [name anyone you have conflict with] heart toward me. Bring understanding, reconciliation, and peace to our relationship. I pray all these things in Jesus' precious name, Amen.

SCRIPTURE REFERENCES

Proverbs 16:7	Matthew 22:39	Matthew 18:18
Romans 12:18 NLT	Matthew 5:9	Revelation 12:11
Hebrews 12:14	Luke 10:19	Proverbs 21:1

25 Prayer to Restore Relationship

HEAVENLY FATHER, I come to You asking for restoration of my relationship with [person's name]. Your Word says that the apostle Paul and his partner in ministry, Barnabas, "had such a sharp disagreement that they parted company." But they later reconciled and continued ministering together. After Jacob stole his brother Esau's birthright, they separated for years but later reconciled. After Joseph's brothers sold him into slavery and he went through thirteen years of extreme hardship, he forgave them, and they were reconciled. Father, You can restore any relationship. Nothing is impossible with You. So, I ask You to restore my relationship with [person's name]. Help us to forgive each other, let go of every offense and hurt, and start anew.

You said, "Do all that you can to live in peace with everyone," and "Pursue peace with all people, and holiness, without which no one will see the Lord." Help me to do everything I can to bring peace to my relationship with [person's name]. Help me to humble myself and apologize, if I need to. Help me to be the bigger person and set the example of love and reconciliation. As

I do my part, I ask for You to do what only You can do and bring divine restoration.

Your Word says, "When a man's ways please the LORD, he makes even his enemies to be at peace with him." I pray that my ways would please You and that You would cause [person's name] to be at peace with me. You said the heart of a king is in Your hands, and like a river You turn it whichever way You wish. If You can turn a king's heart, You can turn anyone's heart. So, I ask You to turn [person's name] heart toward me. I pray he/she would want peace and reconciliation with me. I pray that You would not only restore our relationship but make it better than it was before. In Jesus' precious name I pray, Amen.

SCRIPTURE REFERENCES

Acts 15:39 NIV	Romans 12:18 NLT	Proverbs 16:7
Genesis 32	Hebrews 12:14	Proverbs 21:1
Genesis 45:4–8	Matthew 5:9	

III
PERSONAL PRAYERS

26 Prayer for the Year

Heavenly Father, thank You for another year to live and serve You. I commit this new year to You at the outset and ask You to bless [year] from start to finish. Your Word says, "You crown the year with Your goodness, and Your paths drip with abundance." Crown [year] with Your goodness and make my path drip with abundance. I pray that at the end of this year, I would look back with awestruck amazement at what You did. Your Word says, "The path of the righteous is like the light of dawn, which shines brighter and brighter until full day." Thank You that my path is shining brighter and brighter. [Year] will be my brightest and best year so far—a year of unprecedented favor, explosive blessings on all sides, supernatural abundance, new doors of opportunity, expansion of my territory, and new levels of influence and impact for the Kingdom of God.

Father, I receive Your blessing from the book of Numbers: "The Lord bless you and keep you; the Lord make his face shine on you and be gracious to you; the Lord turn his face toward you and give you peace." Cause Your face to shine upon me this year. Cover me with Your grace. Grant me Your unshakable peace. As Jabez prayed, bless me indeed, enlarge my territory, keep Your hand upon me, and keep me from evil. Thank You that Your blessings are chasing and overtaking me. I can't outrun Your blessings. I am blessed when I come in and blessed when I go out. You are commanding the blessing upon my storehouse and everything to which I set my hands.

Your Word says, "Commit everything you do to the LORD. Trust him, and he will help you." I commit this year and everything in my life to You. I ask You to be with me in a mighty way this year. Help me to wake up every morning with thanksgiving, passion, and purpose. Help me to be a great steward of my time, talents, relationships, finances, and everything You have given me. Guide and direct me by Your Holy Spirit. Give me wisdom in every decision I make, divine strategies and grace to navigate every challenge, favor with everyone with whom I come into contact and everything I set my hands to do, and protection from anything that would try to come against me.

Father, help me draw closer to You than ever before this year and become a better disciple of Christ. Help me to serve and bless others, shine His light, and be His fragrant aroma everywhere I go. Help me to live a surrendered, obedient life that is pleasing to You. As I do, I pray that I would experience greater levels of Your favor, blessings, and impact for Your Kingdom. Thank You that [year] is going to be the best year of my life so far! I pray all these things in the name of Jesus, Amen.

SCRIPTURE REFERENCES

Psalm 65:11	1 Chronicles 4:10	Matthew 5:16
Proverbs 4:18 ESV	Deuteronomy 28:2, 6, 8	2 Corinthians 2:15–17
Numbers 6:24–26 NIV	Psalm 37:5 NLT	2 Corinthians 5:20

27 Prayer for a Blessed Week

HEAVENLY FATHER, Your Word says, "Commit everything you do to the Lord. Trust him, and he will help you." I commit this week and everything in my life to You. I ask You to be with me in a mighty way this week. Help me to wake up every morning with thanksgiving, passion, and purpose. Help me to be a great steward of my time, talents, relationships, finances, and everything You have given me. Guide and direct me by Your Holy Spirit. Give me wisdom in every decision I make, divine strategies and grace to navigate every challenge, favor with everyone with whom I come into contact and everything I set my hands to do, and protection from anything that would try to come against me.

Father, I receive Your blessing from Numbers: "The LORD bless you and keep you; the LORD make his face shine on you and be gracious to you; the LORD turn his face toward you and give you peace." Cause Your face to shine upon me this week. Cover me with Your grace. Grant me Your unshakable peace. As Jabez prayed, bless me indeed, enlarge my territory, keep Your hand upon me, and keep me from evil. Thank You that Your blessings are chasing me and overtaking me. I can't even outrun Your blessings. I am blessed when I come in and blessed when I go out. You are commanding the blessing upon my storehouse and everything to which I set my hands.

Your Words says, "Above all, constantly seek God's kingdom and his righteousness, then all these less important things will be given to you abundantly." Help me to keep You first place and to be Kingdom-minded and not self-minded. Help me to shine Your light and be the fragrant aroma of Christ everywhere I go. As an ambassador for Christ, help me to represent Jesus well and look to serve and bless others, as He taught us to do. Thank You that as I seek You first, everything I desire will come to me in abundance, and I will see new levels of Your favor, blessings and victory. I pray all these things in the mighty name of Jesus, Amen.

SCRIPTURE REFERENCES

Psalm 37:5 NLT
Numbers 6:24–26 NIV
1 Chronicles 4:10

Deuteronomy 28:2, 6, 8
Matthew 6:33 TPT
Matthew 5:16

2 Corinthians 2:15–17
2 Corinthians 5:20

28 Prayer Against Deception

HEAVENLY FATHER, our world is full of deception. The government, news media, and social media are often deceptive. What people present to us is often not who they really are. There is a myriad of scams designed to trick us and steal our money or information. AI can steal people's voices and appearances to deceive. In Matthew 24, Jesus' disciples asked Him what the signs of the end times would be, and the first thing He said was, "Take heed that no one deceives you." He mentioned deception three times in that passage. Timothy says, "Evil men and impostors will grow worse and worse, deceiving and being deceived." Deception is everywhere today.

Thank You that according to John 16:13, the Spirit of truth guides me in all truth and helps me recognize deception. Help me to be sensitive to the Holy Spirit alarm in my spirit when I am being deceived and not to ignore or override it. Give me great spiritual discernment and eyes to see past people's facades and words and know their true character. Your Word says, "Beloved, do not believe every spirit, but test the spirits, whether they are of God." Help me to test the spirits and be careful about who I listen to, allow to influence me, and associate with. Help me to be a person of truth and integrity, not deceiving anyone or allowing anyone to deceive me.

Lord, You gave me authority over all the power of the enemy, and whatever I bind on earth will be bound in heaven. So, I bind, cut off, and cast out every lying spirit, seducing spirit, and demonic spirit from deceiving, tricking, or scamming me in any way, in Jesus' mighty name. I cover my mind with the blood of Jesus, put on the whole armor of God, and stand against the wiles of the enemy. Father, saturate my mind with Your truth and guard my mind from any deception. I pray all these things in the precious name of Jesus, Amen.

SCRIPTURE REFERENCES

Matthew 24:4   John 16:13   Matthew 18:18
2 Timothy 3:13   1 John 4:1

29 Prayer for Breakthrough

HEAVENLY FATHER, I come before You asking for supernatural breakthrough in my life. Thank You that 2 Samuel 5:20 says that You are Jehovah Baal Perazim, the God of the breakthrough. David said, "The Lord has broken through my enemies before me, like a breakthrough of water." You are bigger, stronger, higher, and greater than anything I face. You are a supernatural, way-making, miracle-working, mountain-moving God. Nothing is impossible with You! You said, "I will go before you and will level the mountains; I will break down gates of bronze and cut through bars of iron." Deuteronomy 1:30 says that You will go before me and fight for me. You are leveling every mountain in my path, cutting through every obstacle, and fighting my battles.

Micah says, "The Breaker [the Messiah] will go up before them. They will break through . . . and their King will pass on before them, the Lord at their head." You are the Breaker, and You will lead me to breakthrough and victory. Thank You that when I feel stuck in any area of my life, You have supernatural ways of getting me unstuck. When the Israelites were stuck at the Red Sea with no escape in the natural, You parted the sea, and they walked across on dry ground. You can make a way where there seems to be no way. You make roads in the wilderness, streams in the desert. Thank You that I don't have to fear or worry or try to figure it out because You are with me and for me. Breakthrough is on the way, and victory is certain! I thank You and praise You for it, and it's in Jesus' mighty name I pray, Amen.

SCRIPTURE REFERENCES

2 Samuel 5:20 Deuteronomy 1:30 Isaiah 43:19
Isaiah 45:2 NIV Micah 2:13 AMPC

---

30 Prayer to be a Great Life Manager

HEAVENLY FATHER, thank You for the gift of my life, for all the wonderful people in my life, and for everything You have given me. You have blessed me with so much. Help me not to take anything for granted but to be a great manager of my life and everything You have entrusted to me. You said, "If any of you lacks wisdom, let him ask of God, who gives to all liberally and without reproach, and it will be given to him." I ask for the wisdom and anointing to manage my time, talents, relationships, health, finances, work/business, Kingdom assignment/ministry, and every aspect of my life with wisdom and excellence.

Your Word says, "Look carefully then how you walk, not as unwise but as wise, making the best use of the time, because the days are evil." Help me to be a great manager of my time and not waste time on distractions and fruitless activities You didn't lead me to pursue. I pray as David did, "LORD, remind me how brief my time on earth will be. Remind me that my days are numbered—how fleeting my life is." Help me to make the most of my time on earth, to live each day as if it were my last, and to be laser-focused on fulfilling my destiny.

Your Word says, "Each of you should use whatever gift you have received to serve others, as faithful stewards of God's grace in its various forms." Help me to be a great steward of the gifts and talents You have given me and to be faithful to use them to serve others, further Your Kingdom, and bring You glory. Help me not to bury my gifts and talents out of fear, insecurity, or limiting mindsets but to be like the two servants in the parable of talents who invested their talents and got a twofold return for the master.

Father, I know people are the most important thing to You. You sent Jesus to die on the cross for people. You commanded us to love other people as we love ourselves. Jesus told us to follow His example of washing His disciples' feet and serving others. Help me to be a great steward of all my relationships. Help me to love well my family, friends, and other key people in my life. Help me to care for them, give them my time and attention, and serve them sacrificially.

I pray that I would also be a great manager of my finances, health, work/business, and Kingdom assignment. Help me to make wise decisions, to have discipline and the fruit of self-control, and to be a person of excellence in every area of my life. You said that each of us will give an account for our life on the day of judgment. Make me a wise, faithful, and trustworthy manager of my life so that when I stand before You on that day, I will hear the words, "Well done, my good and faithful servant." I pray all these things in the precious name of Jesus, Amen.

SCRIPTURE REFERENCES

James 1:5	1 Peter 4:10 NIV	Romans 14:12
Ephesians 5:15–16 ESV	Matthew 22:39	Matthew 25:21
Psalm 39:4 NLT	John 13:14–16	

31 Prayer for More Discipline

Heavenly Father, I come to You asking for more discipline so that I can become all You created me to be and live the most victorious life. Your Word says, "Get wisdom, discipline, and good judgment." I ask for more:

- Discipline in my thought life. Help me to have the mind of Christ, take every thought captive, and only think positive, faith-filled, victorious thoughts that line up with Your Word.
- Discipline with my mouth. Your Word says that our tongue is like the rudder of a ship or a bridle in a horse's mouth; it determines the whole course of our life. Help me to only speak positive, faith-filled, edifying words.
- Discipline with my emotions. Your Word says, "A person without self-control is like a city with broken-down walls." Help me to have Spirit-controlled emotions and reject toxic emotions.
- Discipline with my time. Your Word says, "Redeeming the time, because the days are evil." Help me not to fritter my time away on my phone, social media, and other fruitless activities, but to be a wise, disciplined steward of my time.
- Discipline with my finances. Jesus said if we are faithful with a little, You will entrust us with more. Help me to be disciplined and wise with the finances You have given me. Help me stick to a budget, save, and not overspend.
- Discipline with taking care of my body. Help me to eat healthy, not overeat, exercise regularly, and get adequate sleep. Paul wrote, "I discipline my body like an athlete, training it to do what it should."

- Discipline about resisting temptations. Help me not to give in to carnal desires but to walk in holiness and excellence in spirit, soul, and body.
- Discipline about what I look at on social media and other media. Help me to guard my eye gate and mind gate and only feed my mind positive, inspiring, wholesome content. David said, "I will set nothing wicked thing before my eyes."
- Discipline about what I post on social media. Your Word says, "A fool vents all his feelings, but a wise man holds them back."

Father, thank You that the Helper, the Holy Spirit, lives on the inside of me. I have His fruit of self-control, and He will help me have discipline in all of these areas. I pray I would be like Daniel who "distinguished himself above the governors and satraps, because an excellent spirit was in him." He had discipline to refuse the king's delicacies and not to defile himself in any way. Help me to have an excellent spirit and discipline like Daniel in every area of my life so that I can become all You created me to be and live the most victorious life for Your glory. I pray all these things in Jesus' mighty name, Amen.

SCRIPTURE REFERENCES

Proverbs 23:23 NLT
2 Corinthians 10:5
Philippians 4:8
James 3:3-5

Proverbs 25:28 NLT
Ephesians 5:16
Luke 16:10
1 Corinthians 9:27 NLT

Psalm 101:3
Proverbs 29:11
Daniel 6:3

32 Prayer for Wisdom

HEAVENLY FATHER, Your Word says, "Wisdom is the principal thing; therefore get wisdom." It says wisdom is better than rubies and gold or anything else I could want. James says, "If any of you lacks wisdom, let him ask of God, who gives to all liberally and without reproach, and it will be given to him." So, I ask You to give me wisdom liberally. Thank You that Your Spirit who lives inside of me is the Spirit of wisdom, understanding, knowledge, and counsel and that I have access to His wisdom at all times. Help me to seek and apply the Holy Spirit's wisdom and counsel in every decision I make.

Lord, You said, "I will give you a mouth and wisdom which all your adversaries will not be able to contradict or resist." I ask for wisdom and a mouth of wisdom with every conversation and meeting I have. Help me not to speak rashly out of my own mind or emotions, but with Holy Spirit wisdom every time I open my mouth.

Father, Your Word says, "He who walks with wise men will be wise, but the companion of fools will be destroyed." Surround me with the wisest friends, colleagues, and mentors. Bring the right people into my life and keep the wrong people out. I pray all these things in Jesus' name, Amen.

SCRIPTURE REFERENCES

Proverbs 4:7	Proverbs 16:16	Luke 21:15
Proverbs 8:11	James 1:5	Proverbs 13:20

33 Prayer to Know God's Will, Guidance

HEAVENLY FATHER, I come to You seeking Your will and guidance [regarding . . . you can name a particular situation if you want]. I know the safest and most blessed place I can be is in Your will. I ask Your will to be done in my life as it is in heaven. Thank You that You said, "I will instruct you and teach you in the way you should go; I will counsel you with my loving eye on you." I ask You to instruct, teach, and counsel me with Your loving eye upon me.

You said, "As many as are led by the Spirit of God, these are sons of God." Help me to be led by the Holy Spirit in every decision I make. Help me to pay attention to His inner witness giving me peace when something is in Your will or lack of peace when it's not. Your Word says, "Let the peace (soul harmony which comes) from Christ rule (act as umpire continually) in your hearts [deciding and settling with finality all questions that arise in your minds]." Help me to follow the peace of the Holy Spirit and not ignore, explain away, or override it.

Father, thank You that You are not a wishy-washy or vague God. You are a very clear, precise God. You told Noah, who wasn't an engineer or carpenter, how to build the Ark with exact dimensions. You gave the Israelites the precise layout and dimensions of the Temple and told them what furniture to put in it. You even told them what color yarn to use for the ephod. You spoke to Abraham through the stars, Moses through the burning bush, the Israelites through the cloud by day and fire by night, and Gideon through the fleece. I ask You speak to me in clear and unmistakable ways through people, signs, dreams, circumstances, however You will. Make Your will so clear that I can't miss it. Thank You that as I seek and obey Your will in every area of my life, Your blessings, favor, and protection will follow. I pray all these things in Jesus' precious name, Amen.

SCRIPTURE REFERENCES

Matthew 6:10
Luke 22:42
Psalm 32:8 NIV
Romans 8:14
Colossians 3:15 AMPC

34 Prayer for Favor

HEAVENLY FATHER, You said that You surround me with favor as with a shield and a crown. Thank You that Your divine favor surrounds me everywhere I go, with everyone I meet, and with everything I set my hands to. Thank You that I wear a crown of favor on my head that no one can take. Luke says, "Jesus increased in wisdom and stature, and in favor with God and man." I pray that I would grow in wisdom and stature and in favor with You and men.

Father, I am reminded about how You gave Joseph supernatural favor everywhere he went. When his brothers sold him into slavery and he was a slave in Potiphar's house, Potiphar put him in charge of his house and all his possessions. When he was falsely accused and thrown into prison, they put him over all the other prisoners. Then, You gave him favor with Pharaoh, who made him second in command over all of Egypt. I ask for Your favor upon me like Joseph had. Give me a Joseph anointing to prosper and be promoted everywhere I go and rise above every challenge I face. One touch of Your favor is better than a thousand days of labor. Thank You that Your favor will open supernatural doors for me and take me places I could never go on my own. I pray all these things in the precious name of Jesus, Amen.

SCRIPTURE REFERENCES

Psalm 5:12
Psalm 103:4
Luke 2:52
Genesis 39:2-6, 21-23
Genesis 41:38-45

35 Prayer for Joy

HEAVENLY FATHER, Your Word says, "Ask, and you will receive, that your joy may be full." I ask You to fill me to overflowing with Your joy. Help my life to be a reflection of the joy of my salvation and close relationship with You. Your Word says, "In Your presence is fullness of joy." Help me to stay in Your presence, live in a way that attracts Your presence, and carry Your presence with me wherever I go. When others are facing challenges and feeling discouraged, may I impart joy and hope to them.

Father, thank You that Your supernatural joy doesn't depend on circumstances. The prophet Habakkuk wrote, "Though the fig tree may not blossom, nor fruit be on the vines; though the labor of the olive may fail, and the fields yield no food; though the flock may be cut off from the fold, and there be no herd in the stalls—*yet I will rejoice in the LORD, I will joy in the God of my salvation.*" I ask for this kind of unshakable, unquenchable joy. Thank You that it is a fruit of the Holy Spirit who lives inside of me, and I have access to that fruit at all times. I ask for Holy Spirit joy to flow out of me like streams of living water.

Father, help me to "count it all joy" when I face various trials, knowing that the testing of my faith produces patience, which will make me "perfect and complete, lacking nothing." Remind me that the joy of the Lord is my strength. Help me not to allow the cares of this world, trials of life, or people to steal my joy and strength. Thank You for the gift of Your amazing joy. I receive more of it by faith with thanksgiving. In Jesus' precious name I pray, Amen.

SCRIPTURE REFERENCES

John 16:24
Psalm 16:11
Habakkuk 3:17–18
(emphasis added)

Galatians 5:22
James 1:2–4
Nehemiah 8:10

Exodus 14:14
Psalm 138:8

36 Prayer for Peace

FATHER GOD, thank You that no matter what is going on in this world or my life, I can have peace knowing that You are on the throne and in control. You have me in the palm of Your hand. You are fighting my battles, working all things together for my good, and perfecting everything that concerns me. Your Word says, "You will keep him in perfect peace, whose mind is stayed on You, because he trusts in You." Help me to keep my mind stayed on You and not the shifting sands of this this world or my circumstances. As I keep my mind stayed on You and trust You, fill me with Your perfect peace.

Jesus, You are the Prince of Peace, and You said, "My peace I give to you; not as the world gives do I give to you. Let not your heart be troubled." Lord, I am reminded of how You had such unshakable peace that You slept in the boat in the middle of a storm. I ask for that kind of unshakable peace that surpasses all understanding to guard my heart and mind and permeate my entire being. Your Word says, "May the Lord of peace himself give you his peace at all times and in every situation." I ask for Your peace at all times and in every situation. Help me refuse to let anyone or anything steal my peace.

Jesus, You gave me authority over all the power of the enemy. You said whatever I bind on earth will be bound in heaven and whatever I loose on earth will be loosed in heaven. So, I bind every spirit of anxiety, stress, fear, worry, depression, torment, and every demonic spirit from me, in the name of Jesus. I loose upon me the shalom peace of God, in Jesus' mighty name. Let Your peace wash over me and abide with me always. I pray all these things in the precious name of Jesus, Amen.

SCRIPTURE REFERENCES

Romans 8:28	John 14:27	2 Thessalonians 3:16 NLT
Psalm 138:8	Philippians 4:6–7	Luke 10:19
Isaiah 26:3	1 Peter 5:7	Matthew 18:18

37 Prayer to Manage Thought Life

HEAVENLY FATHER, Your Word says that my thoughts will determine who I become and the direction of my life. Every decision I make and action I take begins with a thought. That's why You told us to take every thought captive and to let our minds dwell only on what is true, honorable, pure, lovely, of good report, excellent and worthy of praise. Help me to be great at managing my thought life and not put my mind on autopilot to let it think whatever it wants. Help me to level up my thought life and keep my mind going in a positive, faith-filled, thankful, victorious direction.

Father, I repent for every lie I believed, wrong belief I adopted, and thought that did not line up with Your Word. I ask You to forgive me, cleanse me by the blood of Jesus, and close every door to the enemy. I repent for the sins of my ancestors that may have opened the door to defeated mindsets, mental strongholds, and wrong beliefs. I ask You to forgive their sins and cleanse my family bloodline by the blood of Jesus. You said if any man be in Christ, he is a new creation; old things have passed away, all things have become new. Thank You that I have a new bloodline and lineage in Christ Jesus. Old, limited, defeated ways of thinking have passed away. I break every generational curse off me and my descendants associated with mental strongholds and defeated mindsets, in the name of Jesus. I declare that I have the mind of Christ and only think positive, faith-filled, victorious thoughts based on the Word of God.

Father, thank You that the weapons of my warfare are not carnal but mighty in You for pulling down strongholds. So, I pull down every mental stronghold in my life and cast down every lie, wrong belief, limiting mindset, vexing and intrusive thought, and every thought that does not line up with Your Word, in the mighty name of Jesus. Jesus, You gave me authority over all the power of the enemy, and whatever I bind on earth will be bound in heaven. So, I bind, rebuke, cancel, and nullify every demonic assignment and attack against my mind, in the name of Jesus. I cover my mind and thoughts with the blood of Jesus. Father, Your Word says, "The Lord is faithful, who will establish you and guard you from the evil one." Set a guard around my mind and protect it from the evil one.

Your Word tells me that I am transformed by the renewing of my mind and instructs me to "be constantly renewed in the spirit of your mind [having a fresh mental and spiritual attitude]." Help me to renew my mind and program it for victory every day by filling it with positive, wholesome, faith-filled content. Help me to guard what goes into my mind by avoiding negative or ungodly content. Father, science tells us that 95 percent of our thought life is subconscious. We are not consciously aware of most of our thoughts. Science also tells us that our subconscious mind remembers everything we have seen and that has happened to us.* So, I ask You to go into the deep recesses of my subconscious mind to things that may have happened in the womb or my childhood of which I have no memory. Wash away every painful memory, every lie I believed, every wrong belief I adopted, and every mindset that does not line up with Your Word, by the blood of Jesus. Let Your healing, delivering power and truth invade my mind. You said that You have given me a sound mind, so I pray for a sound, peaceful, healthy mind. Give me the mind of a champion. I pray all these things in the precious name of Jesus, Amen.

SCRIPTURE REFERENCES

Proverbs 23:7
2 Corinthians 10:4-5
Philippians 4:8
Romans 12:2
2 Thessalonians 3:3
2 Corinthians 5:17
Philippians 2:5
Ephesians 4:23 AMPC
2 Timothy 1:7

38 Prayer of Protection

HEAVENLY FATHER, thank You that You are our protector and defender. You alone make us dwell in safety. You are our rock, refuge and fortress, shield and buckler, and strong tower from the enemy. You cover me and my family with Your feathers and hide us in the cleft of the rock. You deliver us from the snare of the fowler and

---

*Olga Blias, "Your Subconscious Mind Creates 95% of Your Life," *Thrive Global.com*, 2025, https://community.thriveglobal.com/your-subconscious-mind-creates-95-of-your-life/.

perilous pestilence. A thousand may fall at our side and ten thousand at our right hand, but it shall not come near us. No evil will befall us nor any plague come near our dwelling. You give Your mighty angels charge over us to keep us in all our ways and bear us up in their hands. The angel of the Lord encamps around us and delivers us from all trouble. No weapon formed against me or my family shall prosper. Our enemies will come against us one way and flee seven ways.

Father, I am reminded of how Satan came to You and said he could not touch Job because You had put a hedge of protection around him, his family, and his possessions. I ask for that same hedge of protection around me, my family, home, finances, vehicles, job/business, relationships, reputation, everything in my life on every side so that the enemy cannot penetrate. Surround me and my family like the mountains surround Jerusalem. Second Thessalonians 3:3 says, "The Lord is faithful, who will establish you and guard you from the evil one." Guard me and my family and everything in our lives from the evil one.

Jesus, You gave me authority to trample on snakes and scorpions and over all the power of the enemy. You said whatever I bind on earth is bound in heaven. So, I trample on every demonic spirit, and I bind, cut off, cancel, and nullify all harm, evil, accidents, injuries, sickness, disease, and every demonic assignment and attack against me and my family, in the mighty name of Jesus. I overcome the devil with the blood of the Lamb and word of my testimony. I cover myself, my family, and our home, vehicles, finances, possessions, jobs/business(es), relationships, reputation, and everything in my life with the blood of the Passover Lamb, Jesus Christ. Father, thank You for keeping us safe and for the victory we have in Christ. I pray all these things in the name of Jesus, Amen.

SCRIPTURE REFERENCES

Psalm 4:8	Isaiah 54:17	2 Thessalonians 3:3
Proverbs 18:10	Deuteronomy 28:7	Luke 10:19
Psalm 91	Job 1:9–10	Matthew 18:18
Psalm 34:7	Psalm 125:2	Revelation 12:11

39 Spiritual Warfare Prayer

Heavenly Father, Your Word says, "Submit to God. Resist the devil and he will flee from you." I submit myself, my family, and everything in my life to You. I resist the devil, and he must flee from me. Thank You that I am seated in heavenly places with Christ Jesus far above all demonic powers. The enemy is under my feet in the spirit realm and subject to me in the name of Jesus. I am fighting the enemy from a place of victory; the battle is rigged in my favor.

Your Word says, "The Lord is faithful, who will establish you and guard you from the evil one." Thank You for guarding me from the evil one and giving me spiritual armor to stand against the wiles of the enemy. I put on the whole armor of God right now—the helmet of salvation, the breastplate of righteousness, the shoes of peace, and the belt of truth, and I take up the shield of faith, with which I quench all the fiery darts of the enemy, and the sword of the Spirit, which is the Word of God. I overcome you, devil, with the blood of the Lamb and the word of my testimony. I cover myself, my family, home, vehicles, finances, possessions, job/business, relationships, reputation, and everything in my life with the blood of Jesus.

Jesus, You gave me authority to trample on snakes and scorpions and over all the power of the enemy. So, I trample on every demonic spirit, and I bind, cut off, cancel, and nullify every demonic assignment and attack against me, my family, or anything in my life, in the name of Jesus. I command every demonic spirit to go from me, my family, and every area of our lives and never come back, in Jesus' mighty name. Father, Your Word tells us not to give the devil any opportunity. I repent for any ways I have sinned and opened the door to the enemy. I ask You to forgive me, cleanse me of all unrighteousness, and close every door to the enemy. I revoke, renounce, cancel, and nullify every agreement and association with the forces of darkness, in the name of Jesus.

Father, thank You that You have given Your angels charge over me to keep me in all my ways and bear me up in their hands. Surround me with Your mighty warring and defending angels to do battle for me in the spirit realm. Put Your hedge of protection around me on all sides that the enemy cannot penetrate. Surround me like the mountains surround Jerusalem. Thank You that You have given me everything I need for total victory over the enemy. I pray all these things in the name above all names, Jesus, Amen.

SCRIPTURE REFERENCES

James 4:7
Ephesians 1:20–21; 2:5–6
Luke 10:17
2 Thessalonians 3:3
Revelation 12:11
Luke 10:19
Ephesians 4:27
1 John 1:9
Psalm 91:11
Job 1:10
Psalm 125:2

40 Prayer to Live a Purpose-Driven Life

HEAVENLY FATHER, Your Word says, "The Lord has made everything for its purpose." You told Jeremiah, "I knew you before I formed you in your mother's womb. Before you were born I set you apart and appointed you as my prophet to the nations." The apostle Paul wrote, "Even before I was born, God chose me and called me by his marvelous grace." Thank You that You are a very precise and purposeful God. You don't create anything haphazardly or randomly. I didn't just show up on planet Earth because my parents decided to get together. I came *through* my parents, but I came *from* You. You knew me before You formed me in my mother's womb and created me with a divine purpose and destiny that only I can fulfill. You carefully chose my gifts, abilities, looks, personality, intelligence, gender, ethnicity, and everything about me for my unique purpose. You didn't create me just to go to work, pay bills, buy some things, take some trips, and die. You have a higher Kingdom purpose and destiny for me to fulfill.

Father, I ask You to show me what my God-given purpose is, the reason You created me. Make it crystal clear so that there is no way I can miss it. Help me to fulfill all my purpose on this earth. Help me not to be like a leaf on a stream just floating along and going wherever life happens to take me but to live a purpose-driven life. I pray I would wake up every day with passion, zeal, and determination to fulfill my destiny. Help me not to waste time and energy on fruitless endeavors and distractions that aren't a part of my destiny. Proverbs says, "A person's steps are directed by the Lord. How then can anyone understand their own way?" Thank You for directing my steps, opening the right doors and closing the wrong doors, putting the right people in my life and weeding out the wrong people, and helping me in every way to fulfill my purpose.

Father, help me to live like Jesus, who said, "Not My will, but Yours, be done." He was obedient even to the point of death on a cross. He said, "I must be about My Father's business." Jesus lived a well-balanced life, but He was always focused, obedient, and disciplined about fulfilling Your will and destiny for His life. Help me to be the same way so that when I stand before You and give an account of my life, I can hear the words, "Well done, good and faithful servant." I pray all these things in the mighty name of Jesus, Amen.

SCRIPTURE REFERENCES

Proverbs 16:4 ESV
Jeremiah 1:5 NLT
Galatians 1:15 NLT
Psalm 20:4
Proverbs 20:24 NIV
Luke 22:42
Philippians 2:8
Luke 2:49
Matthew 25:21

41 Prayer to Represent Jesus Well

Lord Jesus, Your Word says that we are Your representatives on earth. "As He is, so are we in this world." I pray that I would be a great disciple and represent You well in the world. You called us "the light of the world" and said, "Let your light so shine before men, that they may see your good works and glorify your Father in heaven." Your Word also says that we are "the fragrance of Christ" to those who are unsaved and saved. Help me to shine Your light and be Your fragrant aroma everywhere I go. I pray that people would feel the love, joy, peace, compassion, and character of Christ when they are around me.

Your Word says that by this one thing will people know we are Your disciples—if we have fervent love for one another. Not how often I go to church, how many Bible verses I can quote, what I post about You on social media, or even how many good deeds I do. You said love is the number one sign that I am Your disciple. You commanded us to love even our enemies. Help me to practice walking in Your love every day and to love all people, even those who rub my flesh the wrong way and with whom I disagree.

Father, You told us to be holy for You are holy. You said, "Come out from among them and be separate," and "Do not be conformed to this world." Help me not to blend into the world like a chameleon, where people can't tell that I am a Christian, but help me to be holy, stand out, and put my flag up for Jesus. Make me a bold witness for Jesus in this lost, broken, and dark world. Light a fresh fire in me to be more courageous and intentional about sharing the Gospel with others.

Help me to be more like Jesus and live a life that represents Him well and glorifies You. I pray all these things in the precious name of our Lord and Savior Jesus Christ, Amen.

SCRIPTURE REFERENCES

1 John 4:17
Matthew 5:14, 16
2 Corinthians 5:20
2 Corinthians 2:14–15
John 13:35
1 Peter 1:16
2 Corinthians 6:17
Romans 12:2

42 Prayer to Live the Abundant Life

LORD JESUS, You said, "I came that [you] may have and enjoy life, and have it in abundance (to the full, till it overflows)." Help me to enjoy my life and have abundance in every area—impact for Your Kingdom, relationships, health, finances, fulfilling experiences, and every good thing life has to offer. Your Word says, "Those who seek [You] shall not lack any good thing," and "No good thing will [You] withhold from those who walk uprightly." Thank You that You won't withhold anything from me when I seek You and walk uprightly. Help me to do my part and live in such a way that I can receive everything You have for me.

Your Word says, "Eye has not seen, nor ear heard, nor have entered into the heart of man the things which God has prepared for those who love Him." Thank You for the amazing things You have in store for me, which I can't even fathom. Thank You that my path is shining brighter and brighter until the full day. My brightest days and greatest victories are in my future, not my past. You're taking me from glory to glory. By Your grace, I will become all You created me to be, live the abundant and victorious life Jesus died to give me, and fulfill every purpose and plan You have for my life. I pray all these things in the wonderful, majestic name of Jesus, Amen.

> **SCRIPTURE REFERENCES**
>
> John 10:10 AMPC
> 1 John 3:1
> Romans 8:16–17
> Revelation 1:6
>
> Romans 5:17
> 2 Corinthians 5:20
> Psalm 34:10
> Psalm 84:11
>
> Romans 8:32
> 1 Corinthians 2:9
> Proverbs 4:18
> 2 Corinthians 3:18

43 Prayer for Expansion

HEAVENLY FATHER, thank You that You are a progressive God. You want us to keep growing, expanding, and prospering. You never want us to get stagnant. You told Abraham to lift his eyes from the place he was standing, that You were going to give him the land as far as his eyes could see. You told the Israelites, "Enlarge the place of your tent . . . stretch out the curtains of your dwellings; do not spare; lengthen your cords, and strengthen your stakes. For you shall expand to the right and to the left." When Jabez prayed, "Oh, that You would bless me indeed, and enlarge my territory," You granted his request.

Lord, I ask You to expand my territory. Expand my career/business. Expand my influence. Expand my impact for Your Kingdom. Expand my resources. Expand my connections. Expand my support system and community. Help me to live a big life because You are a big God, and I represent You. Expand me so that I can expand Your Kingdom. You told Abraham, "I will bless you and make your name great; and you shall be a blessing." Lord, I desire to be a greater blessing. Thank You that all things are possible with You and that You can do exceedingly, abundantly above all I can ask or think.

Father, deliver me from fear, insecurity, wanting to stay in my comfort zone, limiting mindsets, or anything else that hinders my expansion. Help me to be a fearless, courageous, faith-filled, can-do person who will take new ground for Your Kingdom and glory. I pray all these things in the glorious name of Jesus, Amen.

SCRIPTURE REFERENCES

Genesis 13:14–18 1 Chronicles 4:10 Ephesians 3:20
Isaiah 54:2–3 Genesis 12:2

---

44 Prayer to be a Better Time Manager

HEAVENLY FATHER, I ask You to help me be great manager of my time. David wrote, "Lord, remind me how brief my time on earth will be. Remind me that my days are numbered— how fleeting my life is." Ephesians says, "Look carefully then how you walk, not as unwise but as wise, making the best use of the time, because the days are evil." Help me not to waste time on my phone, distractions, unnecessary conflicts, doing things You didn't call me to do, or being lazy or complacent. Remind me that every day is a precious gift and that my time on earth is short. Your Word says, "You do not know what will happen tomorrow. For what is your life? It is even a vapor that appears for a little time and then vanishes away." Help me to understand that time is my most important commodity, and once it is gone, I can never get it back. I can make more money, but I can't make more time. So, help me to manage my time wisely and make the most of each day. Show me how to structure my days, what to focus on, and what to prune away. I pray all these things in Jesus' mighty name, Amen.

SCRIPTURE REFERENCES

Psalm 39:4 NLT Ephesians 5:15–16 ESV James 4:14

45 Prayer When Walking Through a Trial

HEAVENLY FATHER, thank You that You are always with me, no matter what I am going through. You are the fourth Man in the fire. Like You did with the three Hebrew boys, You're going to bring me out without the smell of smoke lingering on me. Though I am walking through a valley right now, I will not fear because You are with me; Your rod and staff comfort me. You're going to bring me out of this challenging situation with the victory. Your Word says, "The righteous cry out, and the Lord hears them; he delivers them from all their troubles. . . . The righteous person may have many troubles, but the Lord delivers him from them all." Thank You that You hear my prayers and deliver me out of all my troubles.

David wrote, "We went through fire and through water; but You brought us out to rich fulfillment." David also wrote, "He also brought me up out of a horrible pit, out of the miry clay, and set my feet upon a rock, and established my steps. He has put a new song in my mouth—praise to our God." Thank You that You're going to bring me out of this season of trials to rich fulfillment. You're going to bring me out of the pit and put a new song in my mouth. You're going to give me "beauty for ashes, the oil of joy for mourning, the garment of praise for the spirit of heaviness."

Thank You that there is an expiration date on this trial. It is temporary, but Your favor is for life. Help me to take steps every day to feed my faith and keep it strong. Help me to trust Your plan and timing, shake off discouragement and despair, and keep a praise in my mouth, knowing that You are on the throne and in control. Help me to magnify You instead of my problems. Help me not to succumb to fear, worry, anxiety, or doubt, but to have a faith-filled, positive, victorious mindset, knowing that victory starts in the mind. Help me not to have tunnel vision and obsess about my problems but to cast my cares upon You and be anxious for nothing, as Your Word commands. Galatians 6:9 says, "Let us not become weary in doing good, for at the proper time we will reap a harvest if we do not give up." Help me to keep serving You and others while I am waiting for my breakthrough, knowing that I will reap a harvest if I don't give up. Thank You that You always cause me to triumph in Christ Jesus and that in all things I am more than a conqueror. I will emerge from this trial better than I was before! In Jesus' mighty name, Amen.

SCRIPTURE REFERENCES

Daniel 3:19–25	Psalm 66:12	Galatians 6:9 NIV
Psalm 23:4	Psalm 40:2–3	2 Corinthians 2:14
Psalm 34:17, 19 NIV	Isaiah 61:3	Romans 8:37

46 Prayer for Hope, Encouragement

HEAVENLY FATHER, I come to You today in need of hope and encouragement. Thank You that You are the God of all hope. Your Word says, "May the God of all hope fill you with joy and peace in believing, that you may abound with hope by the power of the Holy Spirit." Fill me with joy and peace as I believe You, and cause me to abound with fresh hope by the power of the Holy Spirit. Thank You that You are the glory and lifter of my head. I ask You to lift my head and encourage my heart today. I pray that something would happen today that would encourage me.

Your Word says, "[Cast] all your cares [all your anxieties, all your worries, and all your concerns, once and for all] on Him, for He cares about you [with deepest affection, and watches over you very carefully]." So, right now I cast all my cares, concerns, burdens, fears, feelings of hopelessness, worries, anxieties, sorrows, doubts, discouragement, and depression upon You. Help me to let go of them once and for all. I receive Your promise that You will give me "beauty for ashes, the oil of joy for mourning, the garment of praise for the spirit of heaviness." Like David wrote, You will bring me out of this horrible pit, out of the miry clay, and put a new song in my mouth.

Father, I am reminded that even Jesus needed angels to minister to Him in the Garden of Gethsemane when He was grieved and full of sorrow. Your Word says, "Angels are . . . spirits sent to care for people who will inherit salvation." I ask You to dispatch angels to encourage and strengthen me. Thank You that I also have Your Holy Spirit, who is my comforter and strengthener. I ask the Holy Spirit to comfort and strengthen me and that His fruit of peace and joy would flow from my innermost being like streams of living water. Thank You for giving me fresh hope, encouragement, and strength. Thank You that I can do all things through Christ who strengthens me. In all things I am more than a conqueror, and You always cause me to triumph in Christ Jesus. You will turn every negative situation around and bring me out with the victory! I pray all these things in Jesus' precious name, Amen.

SCRIPTURE REFERENCES

Romans 15:13
Psalm 3:3
Psalm 55:22
1 Peter 5:7 AMP
Isaiah 61:3
Psalm 40:2–3
Luke 22:43
Hebrews 1:14
John 14:26
Philippians 4:13
Romans 8:37
2 Corinthians 2:14

47 Prayer to Let Go of the Past

HEAVENLY FATHER, You said, "Forget the former things; do not dwell on the past. See, I am doing a new thing! Now it springs up;

do you not perceive it?" Thank You that You are always moving forward and You want to do a new thing in my life. I ask You to help me forget the former things and not dwell on the past so that I can lay hold of the new things You have for me.

Help me to be like the apostle Paul, who wrote, "One thing I do, forgetting those things which are behind and reaching forward to those things which are ahead, I press toward the goal for the prize of the upward call of God in Christ Jesus." I make a choice right now to let go of those things that are behind, reach forward to those things that are ahead, and press on toward the upward call in Christ Jesus.

Help me to let go of every past hurt, mistake, failure, disappointment, and everything that didn't work out so that I don't drag those things into my future. Help me not to live life looking through the rearview mirror but to look ahead with faith and expectancy for the wonderful things You have in store for me. You said, "I know the plans I have for you . . . plans to prosper you and not to harm you, plans to give you hope and a future." Thank You that my path is shining brighter and brighter until the full day. My brightest days and greatest victories are in my future, not my past. The rest of my life will be the best of my life! I pray all these things in the majestic name of Jesus, Amen.

SCRIPTURE REFERENCES

Isaiah 43:18–19 NIV
Philippians 3:13–14
Jeremiah 29:11 NIV
Proverbs 4:18

48 Prayer When You Feel Overwhelmed

HEAVENLY FATHER, thank You for always being there for me when I feel overwhelmed. David said, "When my heart is overwhelmed: lead me to the rock that is higher than I." Thank You that You are my rock, refuge, fortress, strength, and a very present help. Just like when David faced Goliath, You are bigger, stronger, higher, and greater than anything I face. You said, "When you pass through the waters, I will be with you; and through the rivers, they shall not overwhelm you; when you walk through fire you shall not be burned, and the flame shall not consume you. For I am the Lord your God, the Holy One of Israel, your Savior."

Father, You said, "Cast your burden on the LORD, and He shall sustain you; He shall never permit the righteous to be moved." You also commanded me to "be anxious for nothing," but to make my requests known to You with thanksgiving. You said when I do that, the peace of God which surpasses all understanding will guard my heart and mind through Christ Jesus. Help me let go, cast my cares upon You, and choose to be anxious for nothing. Flood my heart and mind with Your shalom peace, knowing that You've got me in the palm of Your hand, and everything is going to be okay. You are fighting my battles and perfecting everything that concerns me.

Father, remind me that "I can do all things through Christ who strengthens me." You have armed me with strength for the battle. You said, "Fear not, for I am with you; be not dismayed, for I am your God. I will strengthen you, yes, I will help you, I will uphold you with My righteous right hand." Thank You that You are strengthening, helping, and upholding me. Thank You that Your grace is sufficient for me and Your power is perfected in my weakness. I'm not going under; I'm going over. You are going to bring me out with the victory! I give You all the praise, glory, and honor for it. In Jesus' mighty name I pray, Amen.

SCRIPTURE REFERENCES

Psalm 61:2
Psalm 46:1
Isaiah 43:2–3 ESV
Psalm 55:22

Philippians 4:6–7
Exodus 14:14
Psalm 138:8
Philippians 4:13

Psalm 18:39
Isaiah 41:10
2 Corinthians 12:9

49 Prayer When You Feel Weary, Burned Out

HEAVENLY FATHER, You said, "I will refresh the weary and satisfy the faint." Isaiah 40:29 says, "He gives strength to the weary and increases the power of the weak." I come to You feeling weary, burned out, and needing rest, refreshing, and renewed strength for my spirit, soul, and body. Jesus said, "Come to me, all you who are weary and burdened, and I will give you rest. Take my yoke upon you and learn from me . . . and you will find rest for your souls. For my yoke is easy and my burden is light." Lord, I ask You for rest for my body and soul.

Lord, Your words "take my yoke upon you" is a picture of two oxen yoked together. Thank You that I am not living life on my own. I am yoked together with You. Your yoke is easy, and Your burden is light. Because I'm yoked to You, I can live easy and light. I don't have to live weighed down, stressed out, and exhausted. Thank You that You help me pull the load. Your grace is sufficient for me. Your power is perfected in my weakness. I can do all things through You who strengthens me. You also said, "Learn from Me." Teach me how to live in a way that I can avoid weariness and burnout. Nobody was busier and had more demands on them than You. Everywhere You went, You had throngs of people following You and jealous religious leaders out to get You. Yet, You regularly withdrew to a solitary place to pray and reconnect with the Father. You had regular fellowship with Your disciples and dined with people in their homes. You lived with balance and margin. Teach me to follow Your example. Help me to get great sleep every night, manage stress well, and live a well-balanced life with exercise, fun, community, and fulfilling vacations so that I don't get weary or burned out. Help me not to just grind through life but to enjoy my life.

Father, Your Word says, "Times of refreshment will come from the presence of the Lord." Help me to spend time in Your presence first thing every morning so that I can be refreshed and revived. Thank You for helping me run my race with endurance. I will mount up with wings on eagles, walk and not grow weary, run and not faint. I will live a rich, fulfilling, well-balanced life with a healthy mix of work, rest, and play and avoid the trap of weariness and burnout. I pray all these things in the name above all names, Jesus Christ, Amen.

SCRIPTURE REFERENCES

Jeremiah 31:25 NIV
Isaiah 40:29, 31 NIV
Matthew 11:28–30 NIV
2 Corinthians 12:9
Philippians 4:13
Acts 3:20 NLT

50 Prayer for Rest

LORD JESUS, You said, "Come to me, all you who are weary and burdened, and I will give you rest." Thank You for the promise of divine rest and freedom from weariness and burdens. I ask for Your rest for my mind. Rest for my emotions. Rest for my body. Rest from the stresses and trials of life. Your Word says, "There remains therefore a rest for the people of God. . . . Let us therefore be diligent to enter that rest." Help me to be diligent to enter Your rest. As busy as You were, with throngs of people wanting something from You everywhere You went, jealous religious leaders harassing You, disciples to teach, and a Church to start, You regularly took time to draw away to a solitary place to rest. Help me to follow Your example and live a balanced life with ample time to rest and recharge my battery. Rather than depending on one or two vacations a year to catch up on rest, help me to live a lifestyle that balances my responsibilities with recreation, community, exercise, and rest so that I can run my race with endurance and joy.

Father, help me not to carry burdens I wasn't meant to carry. Your Word commands us to cast our cares upon You and to "lay aside every weight." Help me to do this so that I can live light, fresh, and joyful, not weighed down, exhausted, and burned out.

Your Word says that You give us rest from the day of adversity and that You gave David rest on all sides from his enemies. I ask for rest from my adversities and everything and everyone that has come against me. Calm the wind and waves in my life. Surround me on all sides with Your hedge of protection and shalom peace. Make me lie down in green pastures and lead me beside the still waters. When I lie down to sleep, help me to get sweet, peaceful, refreshing, deep, uninterrupted sleep. Thank You for giving me Your divine rest and refreshing my body, soul, and spirit so that I can be my best for You every day. I pray all these things in Jesus' precious name, Amen.

SCRIPTURE REFERENCES

Matthew 11:28–30 NIV	1 Peter 5:7	2 Samuel 7:1
Hebrews 4:9, 11	Hebrews 12:1	Psalm 4:8
Psalm 55:22	Psalm 94:13	Proverbs 3:24

51 Prayer When You're Waiting

HEAVENLY FATHER, I know we all spend time in Your waiting room, but I confess that I feel like David: "How long, O Lord?" In my flesh, I feel weary of waiting. I ask You to strengthen me, renew a steadfast spirit within me, and help me to trust Your timing. You promised to renew my strength and be good to me when I wait on You.

Hebrews 6:12 says it is through faith and patience that we inherit the promises of God, so help me to have both faith and patience. Your Word also says, "Rest in the LORD, and wait patiently for Him," and "Be still, and know that I am God." Help me to be still and rest in You, trusting that You are working in the unseen realm, moving things into place, and preparing me to receive what You have for me.

David wrote, "My times are in Your hand." Help me not to get impatient and launch out ahead of You in my flesh, but instead wait on Your perfect timing. Help me to let go of control and trust Your plan. I release the need to know when and how. Your Word says there is an appointed time for everything under the sun. Though the vision tarries, it will not be late one second. The manner in which I wait will have a big influence on the outcome, so help me to wait in faith and with a good attitude. Give me the grace to pass the test of waiting. Thank You that in due season I will reap a harvest if I faint not. Thank You that at the perfect time, my breakthrough will come and Your promises will manifest in my life. I pray all these things in Jesus' precious name, Amen.

SCRIPTURE REFERENCES

Psalm 13:1	Proverbs 3:5–6	Psalm 31:15
Psalm 51:10	Hebrews 6:12	Ecclesiastes 3:1
Isaiah 40:31	Psalm 37:7	Habakkuk 2:3
Lamentations 3:25	Psalm 46:10 NIV	Galatians 6:9

52 Prayer to Take Care of Your Temple

HEAVENLY FATHER, Your Word says that my body is the temple of the Holy Spirit. Help me do everything I can to take care of my temple and make choices that will foster good health. You have given me one body to last a lifetime, and You want me to be a good steward of it. James says, "If any of you lacks wisdom, let him ask of God, who gives to all liberally and without reproach." Father, I ask for divine wisdom about what foods to eat and avoid, what supplements to take, and what changes I need to make to become the healthiest version of myself. It was food that caused Adam and Eve to sin in the Garden, so help me to have the Holy Spirit's fruit of self-control with food and not indulge in unhealthy foods. Help me to choose the healthiest foods.

I pray I would have a healthy relationship with food and use food only for its intended purpose—to nourish my body. Help me not to abuse food and overeat because of pain, stress, or boredom. Paul wrote, "All things are lawful for me, but I will not be brought under the power of any." Help me not to be brought under the power of food, alcohol, sweets, or anything but the Holy Spirit. Deliver me from any unhealthy food cravings, addictions, dysfunctions, or bondages. You said the weapons of my warfare are not carnal but mighty in You for the pulling down of strongholds. So, I pull down, demolish, and shatter every stronghold, addiction, craving, and dysfunction related to food, in the mighty name of Jesus.

In Hosea 4:6, You said, "My people are destroyed for lack of knowledge." Help me to constantly grow in my knowledge of nutrition and health. Help me to become an expert in reading food labels, be discerning about deception and marketing ploys on food labels, and be knowledgeable and careful about what I put into my body.

Lord, help me to enjoy exercise and do it consistently several times a week. You made our bodies to move, so help me not to be sedentary but to move my body throughout the day. Help me to lose any excess weight and maintain my optimal weight. As I do my part in the natural, I ask You to put Your super on my natural and bless me with divine health, vim, vigor, vitality, energy, and strength all the days of my life. I pray all these things in Jesus' precious name, Amen.

---SCRIPTURE REFERENCES---

1 Corinthians 6:19–20 1 Corinthians 6:12 Hosea 4:6
James 1:5 2 Corinthians 10:4

53 Prayer over Your Home, Property

HEAVENLY FATHER, Your Word says, "The Lord is faithful, who will establish you and guard you from the evil one." Thank You for guarding me, my family, our home, and our property from the evil one. I'm reminded of how Satan went to You about Job and said, "Have you not put a hedge around him and his house and all that he has, on every side?" I ask for that same hedge of protection, which the enemy cannot penetrate, around me, my family, my home, and my property on all sides that the enemy cannot penetrate. Surround my home, like the mountains surround Jerusalem. Your Word says we overcome the enemy with the blood of the Lamb and the word of our testimony. So I cover every inch of my home—every room, entry point, appliance, possession, and the land on which my home sits—with the blood of the Passover Lamb of God, Jesus Christ.

Father, You promised in Psalm 91 to protect me, my family, and our dwelling. You said You would cover us with Your feathers and we would take refuge under Your wings, that no evil would befall us nor any plague come near our dwelling, and that You would give Your mighty angels charge over us to keep us in all our ways and bear us up in their hands. I ask You to post angels around my home and property to protect us and keep any demonic spirits or evil person from entering. Thank You that You gave me authority over all the power of the enemy and whatever I bind on earth will be bound in heaven. So, I bind, cut off, cancel, and nullify every demonic assignment and attack against me, my family, home, property, vehicles, and possessions, in Jesus' mighty name.

Lord, I ask You to fill my home with Your sweet presence and angels. Make it a sanctuary of love, joy, peace, and laughter. I pray that everyone who enters would feel Your presence and peace. Bless this home, and may I/we make great memories here. Thank You for blessings, peace, joy, favor, and protection upon my/our home. I pray all these things in Jesus' precious name, Amen.

SCRIPTURE REFERENCES

2 Thessalonians 3:3
Job 1:10 ESV
Psalm 125:2
Revelation 12:11
Psalm 91:4, 7, 10–12
Luke 10:19
Matthew 18:18

54 Prayer for Good Sleep

HEAVENLY FATHER, Your Word says that You give Your beloved sleep. You caused such a deep sleep to fall upon Adam that You were able to perform surgery on him and remove a rib from his side. Psalm 4:8 says that You make us lie down and sleep in peace because You alone make us dwell in safety. Proverbs says that when we lie down, we will not be afraid, and our sleep with be sweet. Father, I ask You to give me sweet, peaceful, refreshing, deep, uninterrupted sleep with good dreams. Deliver me from any insomnia, hormonal imbalances, stress, fear, torment, or anything else that would disrupt my sleep.

Lord, You said, "Come to Me, all you who labor and are heavy laden, and I will give you rest." You said in Hebrews 4:9 that there is a rest for the people of God. I ask for Your divine rest when I lie down to sleep. Help me to cast my cares upon You, be anxious for nothing, and experience Your shalom peace. Envelop me with Your presence, love, peace, and protection. Help me to fall asleep quickly and sleep like a baby all night.

Jesus, You said, "I give you authority to trample on snakes and scorpions and over all the power of the enemy," and "Whatever you bind on earth will be bound in heaven." So, I bind, rebuke, cut off, and cast out every spirit of insomnia, restlessness, anxiety, fear, torment, or any other demonic spirit that would try to disrupt my sleep, in the name of Jesus. I cover myself, my sleep, and my dreams with the blood of Jesus. Lord, I ask You to put Your hedge of protection around me and my home on all sides. Give Your mighty angels charge over me and my home to keep me in all their ways and bear me up in their hands.

Lord, if there is any chemical imbalance or other issue with my body disrupting my sleep, I ask You to heal it. You are Jehovah Rapha, the God who heals me. Thank You that I am healed by the stripes of Jesus. I command every cell in my body to be in harmony and balance and to be at rest and peace, in Jesus' name. Lord, if there is anything else causing sleeplessness in my life—prescription drugs, my diet, mineral deficiencies, or anything else—I ask You to reveal it to me so that I can make any needed changes. Thank You that, from this moment on, I will enjoy sweet, divine sleep every night. In Jesus' name I pray, Amen.

SCRIPTURE REFERENCES

Psalm 127:2	Matthew 11:28	Matthew 18:18
Psalm 4:8	Hebrews 4:9	Job 1:10
Proverbs 3:24	Luke 10:19	Psalm 91:11

55 Prayer for Move, Transition

HEAVENLY FATHER, I lift up this move/transition to You and ask You to bless it from start to finish. Thank You that Your blessings chase me and overtake me. I'm blessed when I come in and blessed when I go out, blessed in the city and blessed in the country. Thank You that my steps are ordered by You and You delight in my way. You led me to make this move, and You are going to see it through to successful completion. I ask You to lean into me with Your grace and cause this move/transition to be smooth, easy, and full of Your favor. Thank You that Your grace is sufficient for me. Your Word says, "The Lord bless you and keep you; the Lord make his face shine on you and be gracious to you; the Lord turn his face toward you and give you peace." I receive this blessing upon my move/transition and my life.

Father, Moses said he didn't want to go anywhere without Your presence. I ask for Your presence to go with me every step of the way during this move/transition. You told Joshua, "Be strong and of good courage; do not be afraid, nor be dismayed, for the LORD your God is with you wherever you go." Help me not to have any fear, trepidation, or insecurity but to step into this new season with faith, courage, and expectancy. Help me to settle into my new place quickly and acclimate well to my new environment. Help me to make new friends and connections easily. I pray that after a short time, it would feel as though I have lived there for years. I pray that this new place would be one of divine favor and blessings.

Lord, thank You that You have given me authority over all the power of the enemy. You said whatever I bind on earth will be bound in heaven and whatever I loose on earth will be loosed in heaven. So, I bind, cut off, and cast out all the forces of darkness from this move/transition, in the name of Jesus. I command you, forces of darkness, to stay away from me and not interfere in this move/transition in any way, in Jesus' name. I loose God's grace, peace, joy, favor, protection, and provision upon me and this move/transition, in Jesus' mighty name. I cover every aspect of my move/transition with the blood of Jesus. Father, You said the path of the righteous shines brighter and brighter until the full day. So, I thank You that my brightest days and greatest victories are in my future, not my past. Thank You that this move/transition heralds a new season of unprecedented favor, explosive blessings, and victory in my life. I pray all these things in Jesus' precious name, Amen.

SCRIPTURE REFERENCES

Deuteronomy 28:2–3, 6	Exodus 33:15	Revelation 12:11
Psalm 37:23	Joshua 1:9	Proverbs 4:18
2 Corinthians 12:9	Luke 10:19	
Numbers 6:24–26 NIV	Matthew 18:18	

---

56 Prayer for Upcoming Travels

HEAVENLY FATHER, I lift up my upcoming travels to [name the place]. I ask You to bless my trip from start to finish. Thank You that Your blessings chase me and overtake me. I'm blessed when I come in and blessed when I go out, blessed in the city and blessed in the country. I ask for blessings at every turn on this trip. Cover me with Your grace and give me traveling mercies. I pray that everything would go smoothly and easily, I would make it through the airport with ease, I wouldn't have any delays, cancelations, or snafus with my flights, and my bags would arrive safely. Thank You that this trip is going to be incredibly blessed!

Father, Moses said he didn't want to go anywhere without Your presence. I ask for Your presence to go with me every step of the way from the time I leave my house to the time I get back home. I ask for Your divine hedge of protection around me, my vehicle, and the airplanes I ride on. Protect me from all harm, evil, accidents, injuries, sickness, demonic attacks, and anything that would try to come against me. Protect my family and home while I'm gone. Give Your mighty angels charge over me to keep me in all my ways and bear me up in their hands. I cover myself, my vehicle, home, finances, airplanes, and entire trip with the blood of Jesus. I declare no weapon formed against me shall prosper. Father, thank You that Your Word says, "The Lord shall preserve your going out and your coming in from this time forth, and even forevermore." Thank You for preserving and protecting me everywhere I go.

Father, I ask You to help me get great sleep on this trip. Send angels ahead of me to clean out my hotel room of any demonic spirits and fill it with Your presence. I pray I would sleep like a baby every night and wake up every morning refreshed and ready to go. I ask You to keep me in great health on this trip. Protect me from any viruses, allergies, food poisoning, or anything that would try to come against my body. Help me to be the fragrant aroma and light of Christ to everyone I encounter. Help me to represent You well everywhere I go. Thank You for a wonderful, safe, and fruitful trip in every way. I pray all these things in Jesus' precious name, Amen.

SCRIPTURE REFERENCES

Deuteronomy 28:2–3, 6
Exodus 33:15
Job 1:10
Psalm 91:11
Revelation 12:11
Psalm 121:8
2 Corinthians 2:15–16
Matthew 5:16

57 Prayer for Purchase of Home

HEAVENLY FATHER, I lift up the purchase of my/our new home. Thank You that You promised to instruct us and teach us in the way we should go and counsel us with Your loving eye upon us. You said, "The steps of a good man are ordered by the Lord, and He delights in his way." Lord, I ask You to order our footsteps and shepherd us through the whole process of purchasing a home, including finding the best realtor, identifying the right home, securing financing, negotiating the best price, and navigating inspections. You said, "As many as are led by the Spirit of God, these are sons of God." So, help me/us to be led by Your Holy Spirit in every step of this critical decision.

Father, I ask You to anoint my/our realtor and grant us Your divine favor to find the perfect home for us, negotiate the best price, and navigate through inspections to closing. Help us get the best home for the best price.

Father, You know all things. You know everything about the houses I/we will look at, the neighbors, and the neighborhood. You know if there are hidden defects or other problems with a home. I ask You to guide us to the perfect home for us—a quality home we love that meets all our needs and doesn't have any hidden issues, has great neighbors, and is in a safe, pretty neighborhood with great amenities. Thank You, Lord, that You are perfecting everything that concerns us. I trust You to bless us with an amazing home. Before we move into our home, I ask You to send angels before us to clear out the home of any unclean spirits and prepare it for us. I pray all these things in the precious name of Jesus, Amen.

SCRIPTURE REFERENCES

Psalm 32:8   Romans 8:14
Psalm 37:23 Psalm 138:8

58 Prayer for Sale of Home

HEAVENLY FATHER, I lift up the sale of my/our home. Thank You that You are with me/us, for me/us, and perfecting everything that concerns me/us. I ask You to help me/us to find the best realtor and to anoint her/him to do a great job advising us, marketing the home, negotiating with the potential buyer, and navigating through the inspection. I ask for divine wisdom about how to get the house ready and to make it the most attractive to potential buyers. Draw the right buyer by Your Spirit—one who is financially qualified, loves the house, is easy to work with, and will go all the way to closing—and keep the wrong people away.

Father, thank You that Your favor surrounds me like a shield and You have crowned me with favor. I ask for Your supernatural favor in the sale of my/our home. Give me/us favor with the negotiations, sales price, inspection, and appraisal. I pray it will sell for the highest price to the best buyer.

Lord, I pray for Your grace, blessings, and favor on every aspect of the sale of my/our home from start to finish. Let it be quick, easy, and smooth. I cover the make readies, marketing, negotiations, inspection, and every aspect of the sale of my/our home with the blood of Jesus. I bind all the forces of darkness from the sale of my home, in Jesus' name. Thank You, Father, that You are going to walk with me/us every step of the way through this sale. It's going to go exceedingly abundantly above all we could ask or think. I pray all these things in the precious name of Jesus, Amen.

SCRIPTURE REFERENCES

Psalm 138:8
Psalm 5:12
Psalm 103:4
Ephesians 3:20

IV
MARRIAGE AND FAMILY

59   Prayer for Your Marriage

HEAVENLY FATHER, thank You for the wonderful gift of marriage. You created marriage as the most sacred of all human relationships. It is the only relationship where You said, "The two shall become one flesh," and the only one You compared to Jesus' relationship with the Church. Thank You for uniting [name of spouse] and me together in the sacred bond of marriage and for the love we share. I pray that our love would grow deeper and that our marriage would grow stronger every day. Help us to have a marriage that glorifies You and is a beacon of light and hope to other marriages. Help us to keep You first place in our individual lives and marriage and grow together in our walk with You.

Father, Your vision for marriage is for [name of spouse] and me to become one flesh. Your Word also exhorts us to be in one accord and one mind, and it says that You command the blessing where brethren dwell together in unity. Help [name of spouse] and me to be one flesh, one mind, and in one accord in our parenting, finances, and every aspect of our marriage. May we live together in unity so that we can enjoy the commanded blessing on our marriage. Help us to keep out strife, selfishness, pride, anger, unforgiveness, or anything else that would bring division and undermine our marriage. May we live by Your command that we should "get rid of all bitterness, rage, anger, harsh words, and slander, as well as all types of evil behavior. Instead, be kind to each other, tenderhearted, forgiving one another, just as God through Christ has forgiven you." Help us to be kind and tenderhearted toward one another and be quick to forgive when we hurt each other.

Father, Your Word tells us that husbands are to love their wives like their own flesh and like Christ loves the Church. They are to live with their wives in an understanding way so that their prayers are not hindered. It says wives are to submit to their husbands and respect them. You created marriage and You know best what it takes to have a great marriage, so help [name of spouse] and me to live by these commands. Your Word also tells us to esteem each other as more important than ourselves. Help us to be unselfish and put each other before ourselves. As we strive to live by Your instructions, I pray that we would have a more wonderful, fulfilling marriage than we ever imagined, and one that lasts a lifetime. In Jesus' precious name I pray, Amen.

SCRIPTURE REFERENCES

Genesis 2:24
Mark 10:8-9
Philippians 2:2-3

Psalm 133
Ephesians 4:31-32 NLT
Ephesians 5:22-33

1 Peter 3:7

---

60 Prayer for Wife to Pray

HEAVENLY FATHER, thank You for the amazing gift of my husband and our marriage. Help me to never take him for granted. Help me to be the best wife I can possibly be—the one he deserves and dreamed of when we said, "I do." Remind me that You created marriage as the most sacred and important human relationship. It's the only one where You said the two shall become one flesh, the only one You compared to Jesus' relationship with the Church, and the only one where You said, "What God has joined together, let not man separate."

It's the only one where two people make a covenant with You and each other before witnesses, saying, "For better or worse, for richer or poorer, in sickness and in health, till death do we part." Father, I ask You to always be at the center of our lives and marriage. Help me to put my marriage before all other human relationships, my career, hobbies, and other pursuits. As I strive to keep our marriage sacred and honor my covenant with You and [husband's name], bless and protect our marriage. Cause it to become stronger and better through the years, to be a beacon of light to other marriages, and to glorify You.

Father, Your Word describes a great wife in Proverbs 31. It says, "Her husband can trust her, and she will greatly enrich his life. She brings him good, not harm, all the days of her life." Help me to be trustworthy, to bless my husband, and to enrich his life. It says, "She goes to inspect a field and buys it; with her earnings she plants a vineyard. She is energetic and strong, a hard worker." Help me to be industrious and resourceful, a great businesswoman and manager of finances, and hardworking for my family. I pray that I would use my abilities and talents for the benefit of my family and Your Kingdom.

Proverbs 31 continues, "She is clothed with strength and dignity, and she laughs without fear of the future. When she speaks, her words are wise, and she gives instructions with kindness." Help me to be strong, fearless, full of faith, and wise. Help me to keep joy, peace, laughter, and fun in our marriage and home. The proverb concludes with, "She carefully watches everything in her household and suffers nothing from laziness. Her children stand and bless her. Her husband praises her." Help me to look well after the ways of my household and be a wise steward of everything You have given us. Anoint me to be the best wife and mother I can be. Thank You that my husband will praise me and my children will bless me. Thank You that I will enjoy a wonderful marriage that will grow stronger every year and last a lifetime. I pray all these things in Jesus' precious name, Amen.

> **SCRIPTURE REFERENCES**
> Mark 10:9
> Proverbs 31:11–12, 16–17, 25–28 NLT

61 Prayer for Husband to Pray

HEAVENLY FATHER, thank You for the amazing gift of my wife and our marriage. Help me never to take her for granted. Help me to be the best husband I can possibly be—the one she deserves and dreamed of when we said, "I do." Remind me that You created marriage as the most sacred and important human relationship. It's the only one where You said the two shall become one flesh, the only one You compared to Jesus' relationship with the Church, and the only one where You said, "What God has joined together, let no man put asunder." It's the only one where two people make a covenant with You and each other before witnesses: "For better or worse, for richer or poorer, in sickness and in health, till death do we part." Father, I ask You to always be at the center of our lives and marriage. Help me to put my marriage before all other human relationships, my career, hobbies, and other pursuits. Help me to keep our marriage sacred and honor my covenant with You and [wife's name].

Father, Your Word says, "Husbands, love your wives, just as Christ also loved the church and gave Himself for her. . . . So husbands ought to love their own wives as their own bodies; he who loves his wife loves himself. For no one ever hated his own flesh, but nourishes and cherishes it, just as the Lord does the church." Help me to love, nourish, and cherish my wife as Christ does the Church and as I love my own flesh—because we are *one flesh*. I pray that I would love her selflessly and sacrificially. Your Word says, "In humility consider others as more important than yourselves." Help me to treat my wife's needs as more important than my own. We are told, "Husbands, dwell with [your wife] with understanding, giving honor to [her], as to the weaker vessel, and as being heirs together of the grace of life, that your prayers may not be hindered." Help me to live with my wife in an understanding way and show her honor so that my prayers are not hindered. Help me to be tender, compassionate, and caring. When she needs to talk, help me not try to fix her problem but instead listen with empathy.

Lord, help me to be the spiritual leader of my marriage and family that You created me to be. I pray that I would keep You first place in our home, go to church with [wife's name]/my family weekly, cover [wife's name] [and our children] in prayer daily, and be a godly role model and example to her/them. Help me to represent Jesus well to my wife and family. As I follow Jesus and live by Your Word, help me to keep improving as a husband. May our marriage be a beacon of light to others and bring You glory. I pray all these things in the name of Jesus, Amen.

SCRIPTURE REFERENCES

Genesis 2:24
Matthew 19:6
Hebrews 13:4
Ephesians 5:23–33
Philippians 2:3 CSB
1 Peter 3:7

62 Prayer for Healthy Pregnancy

HEAVENLY FATHER, thank You for this precious child in my womb. You knew him/her before You started knitting him/her together in my womb. You are his/her Creator. Thank You that You who began a good work by bringing this child into conception will be faithful to complete it. Thank You that You are going to protect my child and me through the pregnancy and birthing process, and everything will go perfectly. I ask You to keep my baby and me healthy. I pray that he/she would get all the nutrients he/she needs to develop properly and go to full-term. Bless every aspect of my pregnancy and cause it to be healthy, safe, smooth, and easy. Help me to maintain optimal weight and not have any complications.

I bind, cut off, cancel, and nullify any high blood pressure, gestational diabetes, preeclampsia, anemia, infections, ectopic pregnancy, miscarriages, birth defects, premature birth, or anything else that would try to come against my baby, me, or my pregnancy, in the name of Jesus. I cover my baby, me, and my pregnancy with the blood of the Passover Lamb, Jesus Christ, and declare no weapon formed against my baby, me, or my pregnancy shall prosper. Father, thank You that You give Your angels charge over my baby and me to keep us in all our ways and bear us up in their hands. Thank You that You cover us under Your wing.

Lord, Your Word says that John the Baptist was "filled with the Holy Spirit, even from his mother's womb." I pray You would fill my child with Your Holy Spirit in the womb. I ask that he/she would be a world changer, a history maker, and impact his/her generation for Your Kingdom. May he/she become all You created him/her to be, fulfill every plan and purpose You have for his/her life, and live a life that glorifies You. Thank You for the precious gift of this child and for blessing my pregnancy. I pray all these things in Jesus' precious name, Amen.

SCRIPTURE REFERENCES

Jeremiah 1:5
Philippians 1:6
Isaiah 54:17
Psalm 91:4,11
Luke 1:15

63 Prayer for Your Children

HEAVENLY FATHER, thank You that my children are a heritage and reward from You. Thank You that all my descendants are mighty on the earth and blessed. Thank You that my children are taught by You and great is their peace. They're not only my children; they are Your children. They are Your masterpieces created in Your image and likeness with a divine destiny to fulfill.

Father, I dedicate my children to You and ask You to keep Your hand upon them all the days of their lives. Help them become all You created them to be and to fulfill every plan and purpose You have for their lives. Help them to be world changers, history makers, and impact their generation for the Kingdom of God. Help them to be wise and make good decisions. Help them to say no to temptation and protect them from corrupting influences. Keep them on the narrow path of righteousness that leads to life. Keep the wrong people out of their lives and bring the right people into their lives. You said, "He who walks with wise men will be wise, but the companion of fools will be destroyed." Let my children never be a companion of fools, but surround them with wise, godly eagles. Give them discernment with people and bless them with the best friends, mentors, teachers, and bosses. I pray they would be attracted to and date only godly people with great character. I pray they would only marry the person You ordained for them to marry, serve the Lord with them, and raise godly children.

Father, keep my children safe from all harm and evil. Put Your hedge of protection around them everywhere they go. Give Your mighty warring and defending angels charge over them to keep them in all their ways and bear them up in their hands. You said, "The posterity of the righteous will be delivered," and "if the Son makes you free, you shall be free indeed." If there is anything my children need freedom from, set them free. You said, "Beloved, I pray that you may prosper in all things and be in health, just as your soul prospers." Help my children to prosper in every area of their lives and be in good health, even as their souls prosper. I pray all these things in the all-powerful, matchless name of Jesus, Amen.

SCRIPTURE REFERENCES

Psalm 127:3–5	Luke 11:4	Psalm 91:10–12
Deuteronomy 28:4	1 Corinthians 10:13	Proverbs 11:21
Psalm 112:1–2	Matthew 7:13–14	John 8:36
Isaiah 54:13	Proverbs 13:20	3 John 1:2
Ephesians 3:20	Job 1:10	

64 Prayer to Dedicate Child

HEAVENLY FATHER, I come before You to dedicate [child's name] to You. Jeremiah 1:5 says You knew [child's name] before You knit him/her together in my womb. He/she came through his/her parents, but he/she came from You. He/she belongs to You, and we are just stewards of him/her on earth. So, I dedicate him/her back to You like Hannah dedicated Samuel and Mary and Joseph dedicated Jesus to You. I dedicate his/her gifts, talents, mind, heart, and future to You. Use him/her for Your Kingdom and glory. Make him/her a vessel of honor, sanctified and useful for the Master's use. Help him/her to become all You created him/her to be and fulfill every plan and purpose You have for his/her life.

Lord, You said You wish we were either hot or cold for You, but if we are lukewarm, You want to spit us out of Your mouth. Father, set [child's name] on fire for You. Help him/her not to ever be casual or lukewarm about You. May he/she love You with all his/her heart, soul, mind, and strength, which is the first and greatest commandment. May he/she keep You first place in his/her life and seek first Your Kingdom and righteousness. May he/she be an oak of righteousness, the planting of the Lord for Your glory.

Father, I ask You to keep Your hand upon [child's name] all the days of his/her life. Help him/her to stay on the path of Your perfect will for his/her life. Surround him/her with the godliest and best friends, mentors, teachers, and colleagues, and keep the wrong people out of his/her life. Help him/her marry only the person You have ordained for him/her to marry. Put Your hedge of protection around [child's name] all the days of his/her life. Give Your mighty angels charge over him/her to keep him/her in all his/her ways and bear him/her up in their hands. Thank You that according to Deuteronomy 28:4, the fruit of my body is blessed. My descendants are mighty on the earth and blessed. My children are taught by You, and great is their peace. Thank You for the incredible blessing of [child's name] and that You will bless and keep him/her all the days of his/her life. I pray all these things in Jesus' mighty name, Amen.

SCRIPTURE REFERENCES

Jeremiah 1:5
1 Samuel 1:27–28
Luke 2:22
2 Timothy 2:21
Revelation 3:15–16

Mark 12:30
Matthew 6:33
Isaiah 61:3
Job 1:10
Psalm 91:11

Deuteronomy 28:4
Psalm 112:2
Isaiah 54:13

65 Prayer for Wayward Child

LORD JESUS, thank You that You are the Great Shepherd. You said You would leave the ninety-nine sheep to go after the one who was lost. Thank You that You are pursuing [name of child]. There is no place he/she can run from Your presence. You will never give up on him/her. You created him/her and brought him/her into this world. He/she is Your child, and You love him/her even more than I do. I can trust that You have him/her in that palm of Your hand, no harm will come to him/her, and You will guide him/her to the path of salvation and Your perfect will for his/her life.

I ask You to send Gospel messengers across his/her path to speak the truth in love into his/her life. Open his/her heart, mind, and eyes to the truth, and may the truth set him/her free. Deliver him/her from lies, unbelief, rebellion, [name anything else you've seen, like addictions, etc.], or anything else that has been a hindrance to him/her surrendering his/her life to You. Remove the wrong people from his/her life and bring the right friends and mentors into his/her life. I bind, rebuke, cut off, and cast out every demonic spirit from [name of child], and I break off every stronghold, generational curse, bondage, and work of darkness from [name of child], in the mighty name of Jesus. I cover [name of child] with the blood of Jesus. I declare no weapon formed against [name of child] shall prosper.

Father, like the prodigal son, I pray that [name of child] will come to his/her senses quickly, leave the pigpen, and return to his/her loving heavenly Father and family. I ask You to take what the devil meant for evil and turn it for good in his/her life. Romans 8:28 says, "All things work together for good to those who love God, to those who are the called according to His purpose." So, I ask You to work everything [name of child] has been through for his/her good. Set him/her on fire for Jesus and may he/she serve You for the rest of his/her life. I pray he/she would become all You created him/her to be and fulfill every plan You have for his/her life. I ask all these things in the matchless name of Jesus, Amen.

SCRIPTURE REFERENCES

Matthew 18:12
Psalm 139:7-12
Jeremiah 1:5
2 Peter 3:9
1 Timothy 2:4
Luke 15:11-32
Genesis 50:20
Romans 8:28

66 Prayer for Wayward Spouse

HEAVENLY FATHER, I lift up [spouse's name], who is away from You. David wrote, "Where can I go from your Spirit? Where can I flee from your presence?" Thank You that there is nowhere my husband/wife can go from Your presence. Let [spouse's name] feel Your abiding presence and unconditional love like never before. Woo him/her back to You. With fatherly love, convict him/her of his/her sins, rebellion, and independence from You. Help him/her to totally surrender to Jesus and make Him Lord of his/her life, not just his/her Savior.

Father, You turned Saul of Tarsus from a hard-hearted man who persecuted and imprisoned Christians and approved the murder of Stephen into the apostle Paul, who wrote half the New Testament. You can transform anyone. There is no one beyond Your reach and redemption. You said You would leave the ninety-nine sheep to go after the one that's gone astray. So, I ask You to pursue my husband/wife and transform him/her into the person You created him/her to be. You said, "I will give you a new heart and put a new spirit within you; I will take the heart of stone out of your flesh and give you a heart of flesh." I ask You to give [spouse's name] a new heart and spirit. Turn his/her heart, O God. Remove all hardness, unbelief, rebellion, pride, bitterness, and anything else that needs to go, and give him/her a heart after You.

Lord, You said You've given me authority over all the power of the enemy. You said whatever I bind on earth will be bound in heaven and whatever I loose on earth will be loosed in heaven. So, I bind, rebuke, cut off, and cast out every spirit of unbelief, lying, pride, rebellion, independence, and every demonic spirit from [spouse's name], in the mighty name of Jesus. I command every demonic spirit to loose him/her and let him/her go now and never come back, in Jesus' name. Lord, You said You came to set the captives free and proclaim liberty to those who are bound. So, I ask You to set him/her free from all captivity and bondage. Set [spouse's name] on fire for You, and help him/her to become all You created him/her to be. Thank You that we will have a blessed marriage that glorifies You. You are in the business of transforming lives, and nothing is impossible with You! I pray this in the all-powerful name of Jesus, Amen.

SCRIPTURE REFERENCES

Psalm 139:7–8 NIV
Matthew 18:12
Ezekiel 36:26
Luke 10:19
Matthew 18:18

67 Prayer for Unsaved Spouse

HEAVENLY FATHER, I lift up [spouse's name] to You and pray for him/her to be saved and to surrender his/her life to You. Your Word says You desire that none should perish but that all would come to a knowledge of the truth and be saved. I pray that You would cause him/her to know the truth and be saved. Send Gospel messengers across his/her path to speak truth into his/her life in a way they can receive. You said You would leave the ninety-nine sheep to go after the one that was lost, so I ask You to pursue [spouse's name] relentlessly. Open his/her heart, mind, and eyes to the truth of Jesus Christ. You said, "Do not be unequally yoked together with unbelievers. For what fellowship has righteousness with lawlessness? And what communion has light with darkness?" It is Your will for us to become one flesh and be equally yoked in our faith, so I ask You to move mightily in [spouse's name's] life. Save him/her and set him/her on fire for Jesus. Help him/her to become all You created him/her to be.

Lord, You said You've given me authority over all the power of the enemy. You said whatever I bind on earth will be bound in heaven and whatever I loose on earth will be loosed in heaven. So, I bind, rebuke, cut off, and cast out every spirit of unbelief, lying, pride, rebellion, independence, and every demonic spirit from [spouse's name], in the mighty name of Jesus. I command every demonic spirit to loose him/her and let him/her go now and never come back, in Jesus' name. Lord, You said You came to set the captives free and proclaim liberty to those who are bound. So, I ask You to set him/her free from all captivity and bondage. I call him/her out of darkness and into Your glorious light and salvation, in the mighty name of Jesus. Thank You for saving [spouse's name] and that he/she will become all You created him/her to be. Thank You that we will have a blessed marriage where we are one flesh and worship and serve You together. You are in the business of saving and transforming lives, and nothing is impossible with You! I pray this in the all-powerful, saving name of Jesus, Amen.

SCRIPTURE REFERENCES

2 Peter 3:9   2 Corinthians 6:14   Matthew 18:18
1 Timothy 2:4   Luke 10:19

68 Prayer for Troubled Marriage

Heavenly Father, I come to You asking for healing and restoration of my marriage. Thank You that nothing is too broken for You to repair. Nothing is beyond Your redemption. Your Word says that You hate divorce and that no man should put asunder what You joined together. Help [spouse's name] and me to honor the sacred covenant we made with You and each other when we pledged to love each other "for better or worse, for richer or poorer, in sickness and in health, till death do we part." Help us to be reconciled and have peace and unity in our marriage. Heal, restore, remake, and renew it according to Your vision for marriage. Rekindle the love we had for each other on the day we said, "I do." Remove everything that has gotten between us, and help us to become one flesh, like Your Word says. You are a God of miracles, and nothing is impossible with You!

Your Word says, "Get rid of all bitterness, rage, anger, harsh words, and slander, as well as all types of evil behavior. Instead, be kind to each other, tenderhearted, forgiving one another, just as God through Christ has forgiven you." Father, clean us up and help us to get rid of all strife, division, anger, and ungodly speech and behavior from our marriage. Help us to forgive each other, just as You have forgiven us of so much, and be kind and tenderhearted toward each other.

I repent for my part in our marital problems. I ask You to forgive everything I have said and done that sinned against You and my spouse, cleanse me of all unrighteousness, and help me to be the best wife/husband I can be. I pray that reconciliation and peace would start with me, because I am the only one I can control. You said my spouse can be won over "without a word" when he/she observes my godly conduct. So, let me set the example. Let me be the peacemaker. Let me demonstrate the love of Christ, which is patient, kind, not easily angered, keeps no record of wrongs, bears all things, hopes all things, endures all things, and never fails.

Father, thank You that You redeem our lives from destruction. You give us beauty for ashes, the oil of joy for mourning, the garment of praise for the spirit of heaviness. You turn what the enemy meant for evil to good. Thank You for healing, redeeming, and restoring our marriage. Let our marriage be a testament that nothing is beyond Your unlimited power to heal and restore. Make our marriage stronger and better than it ever was before, and let it be a beacon of hope to other marriages. I pray these things in the all-powerful, healing, restoring name of the Lord Jesus Christ, Amen.

SCRIPTURE REFERENCES

Malachi 2:16
Matthew 19:6
Ephesians 4:31-32 NLT
1 Peter 3:1-2
1 Corinthians 13:4-8
Psalm 103:4
Isaiah 61:3

69 Prayer for Unsaved Family Members

HEAVENLY FATHER, I lift up all my family members who are unsaved or away from You. Your Word says in Acts 16:31, "Believe on the Lord Jesus Christ, and you will be saved, you and your household." So, I ask that every member of my household and extended family would be saved. Your Word says that You desire that none should perish but that all would come to a knowledge of the truth and be saved. So, I pray that You would cause them to know the truth and be saved. Send Gospel messengers across their paths to speak truth into their lives in a way they can receive. Open their hearts, minds, and eyes to the truth of Jesus Christ. I call every one of my unsaved and wayward family members out of the kingdom of darkness into the Kingdom of light, in the mighty name of Jesus.

Father, if You turned Saul of Tarsus, a hard-hearted man who persecuted and imprisoned Christians and approved the murder of Stephen, into the apostle Paul, who wrote half the New Testament, You can transform anyone. There is no one beyond Your reach and redemption. You said You would leave the ninety-nine sheep to go after the one that is lost. So, I ask You to pursue my unsaved family members and transform them into the people You created them to be. You said in Ezekiel 36:26, "I will give you a new heart and put a new spirit within you; I will take the heart of stone out of your flesh and give you a heart of flesh." I ask that You give each of my unsaved or wayward family members a new heart and spirit. Turn their hearts, O God. Remove all hardness, unbelief, rebellion, pride, bitterness, and anything else that needs to go from their hearts and give them hearts after You. Help them to humble themselves, bend their knees to Jesus, and surrender to Him.

I bind, rebuke, cut off, and cast out every spirit of unbelief, rebellion, lying, bondage and addiction, pride, and every demonic spirit from my family members, in the mighty name of Jesus. I command every demonic spirit to loose my family members and let them go now and never come back, in Jesus' name. Lord, You said You came to set the captives free and proclaim liberty to those who are bound. So, I ask You to set my family members free from all captivity and bondage. Call them out of darkness into Your glorious light and salvation, and help them to become all You created them to be. I pray all these things in the name above all names, Jesus Christ, Amen.

SCRIPTURE REFERENCES

Acts 16:31	1 Timothy 2:4	Ezekiel 36:26
2 Peter 3:9	Matthew 18:12	Isaiah 61:1

70 Prayer for Family Reconciliation, Peace, Unity

Heavenly Father, I come before You seeking Your divine intervention for peace, reconciliation, and unity in my family. I first repent for anything I have said or done and any wrong attitudes or heart conditions that I have had that have caused strife, hurt, or division in my family. I repent for times I have failed to walk in the love and peace You commanded us to walk in. I pray that reconciliation and peace would start with me, because I am the only one I can control. Let me set the example. Let me be the peacemaker. Jesus said, "Blessed are the peacemakers, for they will be called children of God."

Father, the second greatest commandment is to love others as we love ourselves. Peter tells us, "Above all, love each other deeply, because love covers over a multitude of sins." Proverbs says, "His glory is to overlook a transgression." Help us to love one another in this family, cover over one another's sins, and overlook offenses. Your Word defines the kind of love You want us to walk in: "It is not easily angered, it keeps no record of wrongs. . . . It always protects, always trusts, always hopes, always perseveres. Love never fails." I pray this kind of love would permeate our family. How can we love others the way You want us to if we can't love the members of our own family?

Father, You commanded us to forgive one another just as God has forgiven us in Christ Jesus. How can we harbor unforgiveness toward our own family members when You have forgiven us of so much? Jesus told us to forgive seventy times seven, meaning unlimited times. So, help me to forgive every member of my family that I need to forgive. Help me to remember they are just human like me. We are all imperfect and need Your grace. Help me to release them and any hurt they have caused me. I pray all the members of my family would forgive one another and be reconciled.

Lord, Your Word tells us to "make every effort to keep the unity of the Spirit through the bond of peace." Colossians 3:15 says, "Let the peace of Christ rule in your hearts." Psalm 133 says, "How truly wonderful and delightful it is to see brothers and sisters living together in sweet unity. . . . Indeed, that is where Yahweh has decreed his blessings will be found." I ask that Your peace which surpasses all understanding would rule and reign in our hearts and in our family. Help us to dwell together in unity so that we can enjoy Your blessings. May our family be a testament to Your love, reconciliation, peace, and unity. May it be a beacon of light to other families and bring You glory. In Jesus' name I pray, Amen.

SCRIPTURE REFERENCES

Matthew 5:9 NIV
1 Peter 4:8 NIV
Proverbs 19:11
1 Corinthians 13:5, 7–8 NIV

Ephesians 4:32
Matthew 18:22
Ephesians 4:3 NIV
Colossians 3:15 NIV

Psalm 133:1–3 TPT
Philippians 4:7

V
FINANCES AND CAREER

71   Prayer for Finances

FATHER GOD, thank You that You are my Jehovah Jireh, the Lord my provider. You promised to supply all my need according to Your riches in glory by Christ Jesus—not *my* riches but *Your* riches, which are limitless. There is no lack, inflation, or recession in heaven. The earth is Yours and the fullness thereof. Everything in heaven and earth belongs to You. You are not limited by my job, my bank account, the economy, or anything else in the natural. Your Word says that even in the day of famine, You will cause the righteous to flourish and have more than enough. You have supernatural ways of providing my needs. You multiplied the widow's oil and caused it never to run dry. You multiplied five loaves and two fish so there was enough to feed more than five thousand people. Jesus told Peter to look in a fish's mouth, and there was a coin in it to pay His taxes. You are my Shepherd; I shall not lack. Thank You that I am Your child and an heir of Your Kingdom. You delight in my prosperity. You give me the power to get wealth. You are commanding the blessing upon my storehouse and on all to which I set my hand.

Lord, deliver me from fear and worry about money and help me to trust You. Deliver me from any trauma or unhealthy mindsets associated with money. Set me free from any generational curses or strongholds of poverty, lack, overspending, and poor money management. Help me to tithe faithfully and be a wise financial steward so that You can trust me with more. Help me to stretch my faith and believe You for increase in my finances. Father, I receive all Your promises of provision and prosperity by faith with thanksgiving. I pray all these things in the name above every name, Jesus Christ, Amen.

SCRIPTURE REFERENCES

Genesis 22:14	1 Kings 17:8–16	Psalm 35:27
Psalm 23:1	Matthew 14:13–21	Deuteronomy 28:8
Philippians 4:19	Matthew 17:24–27	Deuteronomy 8:18
Psalm 24:1	John 1:12	
Psalm 37:19	Romans 8:17	

---

72 Prayer for Financial Wisdom, Stewardship

HEAVENLY FATHER, You said, "If any of you lacks wisdom, let him ask of God, who gives to all liberally and without reproach, and it will be given to him." I ask You for divine wisdom and a great stewardship anointing to manage my finances with excellence. I am reminded of how King Solomon asked You for wisdom before You blessed him with wealth. He needed wisdom to properly manage his wealth. I ask for the same wisdom You gave Solomon. Help me to be skillful at budgeting and financial planning. Give me financial acumen to understand finances at a higher level. Help me to save and invest my money wisely, budget and spend it carefully, and give it generously. Deliver me from any love of money, greed, materialism, overspending, or carelessness with money.

You commanded us in Malachi 3 to bring the whole tithe—the first 10 percent of my income—to Your storehouse, which is the church where I am fed, so that Your church can flourish and do Your work. It says that if I don't give You the tithe, You consider it robbery from You and I am "cursed with a curse." But when I am obedient to give You the whole tithe, You promised to open the windows of heaven and pour out such blessing that I can't receive it all and to rebuke the devourer for my sake. Father, help me to be obedient with the tithe.

And help me to be generous with offerings over and above the tithe—to sow into ministries, help others in need, and be a conduit of Your blessings to those around me. Your Word says, "The world of the generous gets larger and larger; the world of the stingy gets smaller and smaller." Give me a generous spirit and a big heart. Remind me that it is impossible to out-give You. You always give back more in return. You said that if we sow bountifully, we will reap bountifully, but if we sow sparingly, we will reap sparingly. You love a cheerful giver. Help me to be a cheerful giver and sow bountifully with a Kingdom mindset trusting that I will reap a bountiful harvest.

Your Word tells us to learn from the ant, who "having no captain, overseer or ruler, provides her supplies in the summer." Help me to be frugal, live below my means, and be a good saver like the ant, storing up finances for the future and unforeseen circumstances.

Father, make me a wise investor like the two profitable servants in the parable of the talents, who invested their money and got a double return for the master. The master said, "You have been faithful over a few things, I will make you ruler over many things." Help me to be faithful with the finances You have given me so that You can trust me with more—not out of greed, but so that I can be a bigger blessing and sow into Your Kingdom more. As I do my part to manage my money wisely—being obedient with the tithe and generous with offerings, saving diligently, spending carefully, and investing skillfully—I ask You to open the floodgates of heaven in my finances and pour out blessings I can't contain. In Jesus' name I pray, Amen.

SCRIPTURE REFERENCES

James 1:5
Malachi 3:10
Malachi 3:9
Proverbs 11:24 MSG
2 Corinthians 9:6-7
Proverbs 6:7-8
Matthew 25:23

---

73 Prayer over Tithes and Offerings

HEAVENLY FATHER, Your Word says the tithe of 10 percent of all my income belongs to You and is holy. It is not mine to pay bills with. It is not my financial "seed" to sow. It belongs to You. Malachi 3 commands me to bring the whole tithe to Your storehouse, which is the church where I am fed, so that Your church can flourish. It says that if I don't give You the tithe, You consider it robbery from You and I am "cursed with a curse." But when I am obedient to give You the whole tithe, You promised to open the windows of heaven and pour out such blessing that I can't receive it all, and You will rebuke the devourer for my sake. Father, help me to be obedient with the tithe. Remind me that it all belongs to You, and You only ask for 10 percent back. I recognize that I wouldn't have these funds without You. Help me to give You the firstfruits of my income and not my leftovers, as a sign that I put You first and trust that You will make the 90 percent I get to keep go further. I dedicate my tithes to You and ask that You would bless them. Use them to build Your Kingdom and bring You glory. As I bring the whole tithe to You, open the windows of heaven and pour out such blessing that I can't receive it all and rebuke the devourer from me.

And Father, help me to be generous with offerings over and above the tithe—to sow into ministries, help others in need, and be a conduit of Your blessings to those around me. Your Word says, "The world of the generous gets larger and larger; the world of the stingy gets smaller and smaller." Give me a generous spirit and a big heart. Remind me that it is impossible to out-give You. You always give back more in return. You said that if we sow bountifully, we will reap bountifully, but if we sow sparingly, we will reap sparingly. You love a cheerful giver. Help me to be a cheerful giver and sow bountifully with a Kingdom mindset. Remind me of Jesus' admonishment not to store up treasures on earth but in heaven "where neither moth nor rust destroys and where thieves do not break in and steal." As I honor You with my finances and sow generously into Your Kingdom, I ask You to cause all grace to abound toward me, that I always have all sufficiency in all things, and have an abundance for every good work. I pray all these things in Jesus' precious name, Amen.

SCRIPTURE REFERENCES

Leviticus 27:30	Proverbs 11:24 MSG	Matthew 6:19–20
Malachi 3:8–11	2 Corinthians 9:6–8	

74 Prayer to Pay Off Debt

HEAVENLY FATHER, I come to You asking to pay off all my debts. You promised in Your Word that I would lend and not borrow. You said, "Owe no one anything except to love one another." You said, "The borrower is servant to the lender." I don't want to be a slave to my creditors anymore. I want to be financially free. I want to lend and not borrow and owe no man anything but to love him. So, I ask for divine provision and wisdom to pay off my debts.

Father, I am reminded of the story of the widow who could not pay her husband's debts, and the creditors were threatening to take her sons as slaves. Elisha instructed her to gather as many empty vessels as she could, and as she obeyed the instruction, You supernaturally filled each vessel with oil. She was able to sell the oil to pay off her husband's debts and still have money left over. I ask You to give me a divine instruction or strategy to pay off my debts. Help me to hear and obey what You tell me to do, even if it doesn't make sense to my natural mind, as this woman gathering empty vessels. As I obey Your instructions in faith, I trust You to put Your super on my natural and do a miracle in my finances.

You have supernatural ways of providing. You're not limited to my bank account, income, or the economy. Jesus told Peter to go look in a fish's mouth to find a coin to pay his taxes. You multiplied the widow's oil. You rained manna from heaven for the Israelites. You brought water forth from a rock in the desert. You are a miracle-working God, and nothing is impossible with You. So, I ask for supernatural provision to pay off my debts. Cause money to come from unexpected sources. Bring me a harvest on the financial seeds I have sown. Help me to be wise and faithful with the finances I have so that You can trust me with more. Thank You that, as I do my part, You will supernaturally help me to become debt free. I pray all these things in the mighty name of Jesus, Amen.

SCRIPTURE REFERENCES

Deuteronomy 15:6	Romans 13:8	2 Kings 4:1-7
Deuteronomy 28:12	Proverbs 22:7	Matthew 17:27

75 Prayer for Restoration After Financial Loss

Heavenly Father, I come to You asking for restoration in my finances. I repent for any mismanagement or unwise decisions that contributed to my financial situation. Thank You that You are a God of mercy and grace. You don't hold my mistakes against me. Your mercies are new every morning. Every day is a new beginning. I can "come boldly to the throne of grace [to] obtain mercy and find grace to help [me] in [my] time of need."

Father, thank You that You are a God of restoration. After Job lost everything, You restored double what he lost. After David and his men lost everything at Ziklag, including their wives and children, they not only recovered it all but plundered the enemy. In Zechariah 9:12, You said, "I will restore double to you." In Isaiah 61:7, You said, "Instead of your shame you will receive a double portion." In Isaiah 61:3, You promised to give me beauty for ashes. In Psalm 103:4, You promised to redeem my life from destruction. Over and over, Your Word declares that You are a God of restoration and redemption. You always restore better than we had before. So, I ask You to restore everything that has been lost and stolen in my finances at least twofold. You said in Proverbs that when the thief is found, he must restore sevenfold. So, I ask You to make the devil restore from his coffers everything he stole from me sevenfold.

Father, thank You that You are not a God of poverty and lack but a God of prosperity and abundance. You placed Adam and Eve in a lush Garden full of abundance where they lacked for nothing. You led the Israelites to the Promised Land, which You described as "a land in which you will eat bread without scarcity, in which you will lack nothing." You said in Deuteronomy 8:18 that You give us the power to get wealth. You said You wish above all things that we prosper and be in good health, even as our soul prospers. Psalm 34:10 says, "The young lions lack and suffer hunger; but those who seek the LORD shall not lack any good thing." Psalm 23:1 says, "The Lord is my shepherd; I shall not [lack]." So, Father, I thank You that You want me to prosper and have abundance and You want to restore my finances. I receive it all by faith with thanksgiving. It's in Jesus' mighty name I pray, Amen.

> **SCRIPTURE REFERENCES**
> Lamentations 3:22–23
> Hebrews 4:16
> Job 42:10
> 1 Samuel 30:18–20
> Zechariah 9:12
> Isaiah 61:7 NIV
> Isaiah 61:3
> Psalm 103:4
> Proverbs 6:31
> Deuteronomy 8:9
> Deuteronomy 8:18
> 3 John 2
> Psalm 34:10
> Psalm 23:1

76 Prayer for Investments

HEAVENLY FATHER, Ecclesiastes 11:2 says, "Invest in seven ventures, yes, in eight; you do not know what disaster may come upon the land." I ask for the knowledge, understanding, and anointing to be a great investor, and the anointing to acquire and manage wealth. You told Abraham, "I will bless you . . . and you shall be a blessing," and he became wealthy. Galatians 3:29 says that I am an heir according to that promise. You said You would give us the power to get wealth, and "a good man leaves an inheritance to his children's children." Help me to make wise investments that will allow me to fund the Kingdom, bless others, and leave an inheritance for my children's children.

Father, I'm reminded of the parable of the talents where You said, "Well done, good and faithful servant" to the two servants who invested their money and got a double return. But to the servant who buried his money in the ground because of fear and got no return, You said, "You wicked and lazy servant." Lord, help me to be like the two profitable servants who invested their money wisely and got a double return for Your Kingdom and Your glory. Help me not to bury my money like the unprofitable servant because of fear, insecurity, or limiting mindsets.

Your Word says, "If any of you lacks wisdom, let him ask of God, who gives to all liberally and without reproach, and it will be given to him." I ask You for supernatural wisdom in choosing the right investments and managing them. You said, "The LORD will send a blessing on your barns and on everything you put your hand to. . . . The LORD will grant you abundant prosperity . . . and [will] bless all the work of your hands. You will lend to many nations but will borrow from none." Thank You that You're going to bless my investments and grant me abundant prosperity. Thank You that everything I set my hands to is blessed. I will lend and not borrow. Thank You that You are going to anoint me to be a great investor so that I can fund Kingdom ministries and be a conduit of Your blessings to others. I pray all these things in the mighty name of Jesus, Amen.

SCRIPTURE REFERENCES

Ecclesiastes 11:2 NIV
Genesis 12:2
Galatians 3:29

Deuteronomy 8:18
Proverbs 13:22
Matthew 25:14–30

James 1:5
Deuteronomy 28:8, 11–12 NIV

77. Prayer for a Job

HEAVENLY FATHER, I come to You lifting up my need for a job. Thank You that You know the plans You have for me, plans to prosper me and not to harm me, plans to give me hope and a future. You are my Shepherd, I shall not lack. You supply all my needs. You take care of the ravens and clothe the lilies with majesty. How much more do You care about me?

Lord, You said, "The steps of a good man are ordered by the LORD, and He delights in his way." Order my footsteps to the perfect job for me. Intersect my path with the right person who has a key to my destiny. Open a door that no man can close, and close every wrong door. Give me supernatural favor and anointing in the interview process. Help me to have a great rapport with the interviewer, and give me a mouth of wisdom to have the best answers. Cause me to rise to the top, even if I'm not the most qualified. According to Psalm 5:12, I declare that Your favor surrounds me like a shield.

Father, Your Word says, "Ask, and it will be given to you." I ask for a great job with great pay, great benefits, and a great boss and coworkers. A job I love and look forward to going to every day. A job that utilizes my gifts and talents to the full. A job with a positive, uplifting, godly environment where there's no drama, politics, gossip, or undermining. A job where I am celebrated and empowered. Father, I ask for a dream job where I can soar and become all You created me to be. I pray all these things in the mighty name of Jesus, Amen.

SCRIPTURE REFERENCES

Jeremiah 29:11
Psalm 23:1
Philippians 4:19
Luke 12:24
Matthew 6:28–30
Psalm 37:23
Revelation 3:7–8
Psalm 5:12
Matthew 7:7
Matthew 21:22

78 Prayer for Favor, Promotion at Work

Heavenly Father, I come to You asking for Your divine favor and promotion in my job. Thank You that You surround me with favor as with a shield and crown me with Your favor. I have supernatural favor with my boss, coworkers, and everyone I encounter and everything I set my hands to do. Your Word says, "The Lord will command the blessing on . . . all to which you set your hand." Thank You that there is a commanded blessing on everything I set my hands to do. Luke 2:52 says, "Jesus increased in wisdom and stature, and in favor with God and man." Help me to grow in wisdom and stature at work and in favor with You and my superiors, coworkers, and the people I serve.

Father, You gave Joseph divine favor everywhere he went, even in adverse circumstances. When his brothers sold him into slavery and he was a slave in Potiphar's house, Potiphar put him in charge of his house and all his possessions. When he was falsely accused and thrown into prison, he was put in charge of the other prisoners. Then You gave him favor with Pharaoh, who made him second in command over all of Egypt. I ask for the anointing and favor of Joseph for influence, promotion, and prosperity. Your Word says promotion does not come from my boss or anyone on earth but from You alone. You put down one and raise up another. Help me to have a spirit of excellence in my job, grow in knowledge and skill, and be faithful and diligent so that You can promote me. Thank You that Your hand is upon me and You have anointed me to excel and prosper at work. Favor, increase, and promotion are in my future! I pray all these things in the precious name of Jesus, Amen.

SCRIPTURE REFERENCES

Psalm 5:12
Psalm 103:4
Deuteronomy 28:8
Luke 2:52
Genesis 39:2–6; 21–23
Genesis 41:38–45
Psalm 75:6–7

79 Prayer for Peace, Protection at Work

HEAVENLY FATHER, I come to You asking for Your divine peace and protection at work. Give me peace with my boss, coworkers, and the people I serve. Fill my workplace with Your presence and shalom peace, which surpasses all understanding. You said when a person's ways are pleasing to You, You make even his enemies to be at peace with him. I pray that my ways would please You and that You would cause everyone to be at peace with me. I ask You to protect me from politics, jealousy, competition, strife, division, discrimination, or anything that would try to come against me at work. You said You would cover me under Your feathers. You said You would hide me in the secret place of Your presence from the plots of man and in Your pavilion from the strife of tongues. You said no weapon formed against me would prosper. You said every tongue that rises against me would be proven wrong. You said You would give Your angels charge over me to keep me in all my ways and bear me up in their hands. I ask You to dispatch mighty angels into my workplace to protect me from any forces of darkness that would try to cause me any trouble at work.

Lord, thank You that You have given me authority over all the power of the enemy. You said whatever I bind on earth will be bound in heaven and whatever I loose on earth will be loosed in heaven. So, I bind, rebuke, cut off, and cast out every spirit of strife, division, jealousy, competition, politics, gossip, slander, discrimination, control, Jezebel, and every other demonic spirit that would try to operate against me at work, in the name of Jesus. I loose upon my boss, coworkers, and workplace peace, unity, and mutual respect, in Jesus' name. I cover me, my boss, coworkers, and workplace with the blood of Jesus. I overcome you, devil, with the blood of the Lamb and the word of my testimony.

Father, thank You that my work environment will be a peaceful, pleasant place where I can excel, prosper, and my gifts can be used to the full. Thank You that I have divine peace, favor, and protection with my boss, coworkers, and everyone with whom I come into contact. Your blessings are chasing me and overtaking me, and You always lead me to triumph in Christ Jesus. I pray all these things in the precious name of Jesus, Amen.

SCRIPTURE REFERENCES

Proverbs 16:7	Psalm 91:11	Deuteronomy 28:1–2
Psalm 91:4	Luke 10:19	2 Corinthians 2:14
Psalm 31:20	Matthew 18:18	
Isaiah 54:17	Revelation 12:11	

80 Prayer to Start a Business

HEAVENLY FATHER, Ecclesiastes 11:2 says, "Invest in seven ventures, yes, in eight; you do not know what disaster may come upon the land." Father, I feel a stirring in my spirit to do what this Scripture verse says and start a business. If that stirring is from You, I ask You to confirm it in unmistakable ways. I only want to do Your will in my life. If it is Your will for me to start a business, I ask You to give me the faith, courage, wisdom, and grace to do it. Help me to have a bold, fearless faith because You said without faith it is impossible to please You and that the just shall live by faith. I pray that I would take a step of faith to start a business in Your perfect timing. When You give me the green light, help me launch out and not be held back by fear, insecurity, or overthinking.

Father, Your Word says, "If any of you lacks wisdom, let him ask of God, who gives to all liberally and without reproach, and it will be given to him." I ask You for supernatural wisdom in every decision I make about the starting of this business. Help me to have great discernment with people and choose the right people to partner with and employ. Help me to seek wise counsel from people who have more knowledge and experience than me, for You said, "In the multitude of counselors there is safety." You said, "I will instruct you and teach you in the way you should go; I will counsel you with my loving eye." So, I ask You to instruct, teach, and guide me every step of the way. Give me creative, cutting-edge, God ideas and problem-solving strategies.

Father, You said that You would command the blessing on my storehouse and everything I set my hands to. So, I ask You to bless and prosper the work of my hands. You said Your favor surrounds me like a shield and that You have crowned me with favor. Thank You that I have supernatural favor with everything I set my hands to and everyone I encounter. Your Word says, "The Lord is faithful, who will establish you and guard you from the evil one." Lord, establish me in this new business and guard me, my business, finances, family, and everything in my life from the evil one. I cover this business with the blood of Jesus and dedicate it to You. I pray that it will help further Your Kingdom and bring You maximum glory. I pray all these things in Jesus' mighty name, Amen.

SCRIPTURE REFERENCES

Ecclesiastes 11:2 NIV	Proverbs 11:14	Psalm 103:4
Hebrews 11:6	Psalm 32:8 NIV	2 Thessalonians 3:3
Romans 1:17	Deuteronomy 28:8, 12	
James 1:5	Psalm 5:12	

81 Prayer over Existing Business(es)

HEAVENLY FATHER, thank You for blessing me with my business and everything in my life. Thank You for every opportunity and the wisdom, business acumen, ideas, contacts, and everything You have given me. Every good gift comes from You, the Father of lights. I dedicate my business to You. Everything I have belongs to You; I am just the steward. Father, You said that You would command the blessing on my storehouse and everything I set my hands to. So, I ask You to bless and prosper my business. Like Jabez prayed, "Bless me indeed, and enlarge my territory, that Your hand would be with me." Cause my business to explode so that I can bless more people, sow more into Your Kingdom, and bring You glory. You said Your favor surrounds me like a shield and that You have crowned me with favor. Thank You that I have supernatural favor with everything I set my hands to do and everyone I encounter.

Father, Your Word says, "If any of you lacks wisdom, let him ask of God, who gives to all liberally and without reproach, and it will be given to him." I ask You for supernatural wisdom in every decision I make in my business, finances, and relationships. Help me to have great discernment with people and choose the right people to partner with and employ. Help me to seek wise counsel from people who have more knowledge and experience than me. You said, "In the multitude of counselors there is safety." You said, "I will instruct you and teach you in the way you should go; I will counsel you with my loving eye." So, I ask You to instruct, teach, and guide me every step of the way. Give me creative, cutting-edge God ideas and problem-solving strategies. Give me uncommon business and financial acumen.

Father, thank You that no matter what is going on with the world, economy, or my bank account, You are my source and provider. You promised in Psalm 37:19 that even in the day of famine, the righteous will have more than enough. Isaac sowed in the land during a famine and reaped a hundredfold because You blessed him. So, thank You that my business and finances will prosper regardless of external circumstances. Help me to keep my eyes on You and believe for it. Your Word says, "The Lord is faithful, who will establish you and guard you from the evil one." Lord, establish me in my business and guard me, my business, finances, family, and everything in my life from the evil one. I cover my business with the blood of Jesus and bind all the forces of darkness from it, in Jesus' mighty name. Father, thank You for blessing and protecting my business and causing it to abound for Your glory. I pray all these things in Jesus' precious name, Amen.

SCRIPTURE REFERENCES

James 1:17	Psalm 103:4	Psalm 37:19
Deuteronomy 28:8, 12	James 1:5	Genesis 26:1, 12
1 Chronicles 4:10	Proverbs 11:14	2 Thessalonians 3:3
Psalm 5:12	Psalm 32:8 NIV	

VI
HEALING THE BODY

82 General Prayer for Healing

HEAVENLY FATHER, I come to You asking for complete healing from [name or describe the condition]. Thank You that You are my Healer and Deliverer. In Exodus 15:26, You said, "I am the Lord who heals you." You connected Your name and identity with healing. You said, "I will take sickness away from the midst of you." You said Jesus bore my sicknesses and infirmities upon Himself at the cross, and by His stripes I was healed. You said, "Forget not all [My] benefits: who forgives all your iniquities, who heals *all* your diseases." Thank You that You are a miracle-working, mountain-moving, way-making, promise-keeping God and nothing is impossible with You! You are bigger, higher, stronger, and greater than this sickness [name or describe the condition]. This sickness is no match for You! You use doctors and medicine, but You are not limited to them. You alone are my Healer, and You can do what doctors and medicine can't do.

I ask You to touch me from the top of my head to the bottom of my feet with Your *dunamis*, miracle-working, healing power. Wipe out every sickness, disease, medical condition, infection, symptom, and anything else attacking my body. Restore me to complete health, vim, vigor, vitality, energy, and strength by the shed blood of Jesus and by the power of the Holy Spirit. Lord, You said in Matthew 21:21 that if I have faith and do not doubt, I can do the same thing You did to the fig tree when You cursed it and it withered and died. You said that I can command a mountain to be removed, and if I don't doubt, it will be done. So, I curse [name or describe condition] at the root and command it to leave my body and never come back, in Jesus' name. I command healing, wholeness, and restoration to every organ, gland, tissue, cell, bone, muscle ligament, tendon, eye, ear, blood, and every part of my body in the mighty name of Jesus and cover my body with the blood of Jesus. I bind, cut off, cancel, and nullify every demonic assignment and attack against my body, in the name of Jesus.

Father, I repent for all the sins of my ancestors and any dietary or lifestyle habits they had that may have opened the door to a generational curse of this health condition [name condition if you know it]. I break every generational curse and genetic weakness associated with this condition [name condition if you know it] or any other disease or sickness off me and my descendants, in the mighty name of Jesus. I declare that we have a new bloodline and lineage in Christ Jesus free from [name condition if you know it] or any other health issues. Father, I know that sometimes the miracle is in the instruction. So, I ask You to show me if I need to make any changes to my diet, lifestyle, exercise, supplements, or any other area that will foster healing in my body. Help me to do my part to take care of my temple as I trust You to do Your part in the supernatural. Thank You that healing is my bread, my inheritance. I receive my complete healing by faith with thanksgiving and declare that I will live the rest of my days in the divine health that Jesus died to give me. I pray all these things in the all-powerful, healing name of Jesus, Amen.

SCRIPTURE REFERENCES

Exodus 15:26
Exodus 23:25
Isaiah 53:4–5
Matthew 8:17
Psalm 103:2–3 (emphasis added)
Matthew 21:21
Mark 11:23
Luke 10:19
Matthew 18:18

83 Healing from Cancer

HEAVENLY FATHER, I come to You asking for complete healing from [name type of cancer]. Thank You that You are my Healer and Deliverer. In Exodus 15:26, You said, "I am the Lord who heals you." You connected Your name and identity with healing. You said, "I will take sickness away from the midst of you." You said Jesus bore my sicknesses and infirmities upon Himself at the cross, and by His stripes I was healed. You said, "Forget not all His benefits: who forgives all your iniquities, who heals *all* your diseases." You said no weapon formed against me would prosper. This cancer may be a weapon that formed against me, but it will not prosper. With long life, You will satisfy me and show me Your salvation. I will live and not die to declare Your works. These are all promises from Your Word, which cannot fail. You watch over Your Word to perform it, and it will not return unto You void. Thank You that You are a miracle-working, mountain-moving, way-making, promise-keeping God, and nothing is impossible with You. You are bigger, higher, stronger, and greater than cancer. Cancer is no match for You! You use doctors and medicine, but You are not limited to them. You alone are my Healer, and You can do what doctors and medicine can't do.

Father, I ask You to cover me from the top of my head to the bottom of my feet with Your *dunamis*, miracle-working, healing power. Wipe out every trace of cancer from my body and restore my health completely. I speak healing, wholeness, and restoration over every organ, gland, tissue, cell, blood, bone, muscle, and every part of my body and cover my body with the healing, delivering, sanctifying blood of the Lord Jesus Christ. Lord, You said in Matthew 21:21 that if I have faith and do not doubt, I can do the same thing You did to the fig tree when You cursed it and it withered and died. You said that I can command a mountain to be removed, and if I don't doubt, it will be done. So, I curse every cancer cell in my body at the root, like Jesus cursed the fig tree, and I command it to wither and die, bear no more fruit, and be flushed out of my body, in Jesus' mighty name! I speak to every cancer cell and tumor and command them to leave my body now and never come back, in Jesus' name! I bind, cut off, cancel, and nullify every demonic assignment and attack against my body, in the name of Jesus!

Father, thank You that Jesus is the name above all names, including the name cancer, and every name must bow at the name of Jesus. So, I command cancer to bow at the name of Jesus and leave my body now, in Jesus' name. Nahum 1:9 says, "He will make an utter end of it. Affliction will not rise up a second time." So, Lord, I ask You to make an utter end of this cancer and that it would never show up in my body again. Father, I know that sometimes the miracle is in the instruction. So, I ask You to give me divine wisdom and guidance regarding my diet, lifestyle, exercise, supplements, alternative treatments, or anything else that will foster healing in my body. Help me to do my part to take care of my temple as I trust You to do Your part in the supernatural. Thank You that healing is my bread, my inheritance. I receive my complete healing by faith with thanksgiving and declare that I will live the rest of my days in the divine health that Jesus died to give me. I pray all these things in the all-powerful, healing name of Jesus, Amen.

SCRIPTURE REFERENCES

Exodus 15:26	Isaiah 54:17	Mark 11:23
Exodus 23:25	Psalm 91:16	Luke 10:19
Isaiah 53:4–5	Psalm 118:17	Matthew 18:18
Matthew 8:17	Jeremiah 1:12	Philippians 2:10
Psalm 103:2–3	Isaiah 55:11	Nahum 1:9
(emphasis added)	Matthew 21:21	

84 Prayer for Cancer Treatment

HEAVENLY FATHER, I lift up my cancer treatment and ask that You would use it to facilitate healing in my body. I ask You to give my doctors supernatural wisdom, revelation, and anointing to provide me the very best care. I pray that any chemo, radiation, immunotherapy, clinical trials, or other treatments would work efficiently and effectively to kill every cancer cell in my body without causing any adverse side effects. Protect me from nausea, fatigue, discomfort, and other side effects. Make every healthy cell in my body impervious to the treatments and cause the treatments to only affect the cancer cells. I cover every healthy cell in my body with the blood of Jesus and declare that no chemo, radiation, or other treatment will damage the good cells, in Jesus' name. No weapon formed against my good cells, tissues, organs, and blood will prosper. Father, I ask You to give me supernatural grace, peace, and strength with all my treatments and make them smooth and easy, yet maximally effective.

As I do these treatments in the natural, I ask You to do the supernatural and wipe out every trace of cancer from my body. Doctors treat, but You alone are our healer. You use doctors and medicine, but You are not limited to them. You can do what doctors and medicine can't do. So, I ask You to use whatever means You will in the natural and supernatural to heal me completely and restore my health. I pray these things in the healing, delivering, restoring name of the Lord Jesus Christ, Amen.

SCRIPTURE REFERENCES

Luke 11:9   Isaiah 54:17   Revelation 12:11

85 Healing from Heart Disease

HEAVENLY FATHER, I come to You asking for complete healing from heart disease. Thank You that You are my Healer and Deliverer. In Exodus 15:26, You said, "I am the Lord who heals you." You connected Your name and identity with healing. You said, "I will take sickness away from the midst of you." You said Jesus bore my sicknesses and infirmities upon Himself at the cross and by His stripes I was healed. You said, "Forget not all His benefits: who forgives all your iniquities, who heals *all* your diseases." Thank You that You are a miracle-working, mountain-moving, way-making, promise-keeping God, and nothing is impossible with You. You are bigger, higher, stronger, and greater than heart disease. Heart disease is no match for You! You use doctors and medicine, but You are not limited to them. You alone are my healer, and You can do what doctors and medicine can't do.

I ask You to touch me from the top of my head to the bottom of my feet with Your *dunamis*, miracle-working, healing power. Wipe out every sickness, disease, medical condition, infection, symptom, and anything else attacking my body. Restore me to complete health, vim, vigor, vitality, energy, and strength by the shed blood of Jesus and power of the Holy Spirit. Lord, You said in Matthew 21:21 that if I have faith and do not doubt, I can do the same thing You did to the fig tree when You cursed it and it withered and died. You said that I can command a mountain to be removed, and if I don't doubt, it will be done. So, I curse heart disease at the root and command it to leave my body and never come back, in Jesus' name. I command healing, wholeness, and restoration to my heart, blood vessels, and every organ, gland, tissue, cell, blood, and part of my body, in the mighty name of Jesus, and cover my body with the blood of Jesus. I speak to every plaque or blockage in my arteries and command them to dissolve and leave my body, in the name of Jesus! I speak strength to my heart muscle and command it to beat normally and function perfectly the way God designed it, in the name of Jesus. I bind, cut off, cancel, and nullify every demonic assignment and attack against my body, in the name of Jesus.

Father, I repent for all the sins of my ancestors and any dietary or lifestyle habits they had that may have opened the door to a generational curse of heart disease. I break every generational curse and genetic weakness associated with heart disease or any other disease or sickness off me and my descendants, in the mighty name of Jesus. I declare that we have a new bloodline and lineage in Christ Jesus, free from heart disease or any other health issues. Father, I know that sometimes the miracle is in the instruction. So, I ask You to show me if I need to make any changes to my diet, lifestyle, exercise, supplements, or any other area that will foster healing in my body. Help me to do my part to take care of my temple as I trust You to do Your part in the supernatural. Thank You that healing is my bread, my inheritance. I receive my complete healing by faith with thanksgiving and declare that I will live the rest of my days in the divine health that Jesus died to give me. I pray all these things in the all-powerful, healing name of Jesus, Amen.

SCRIPTURE REFERENCES
Exodus 15:26
Exodus 23:25
Isaiah 53:4-5
Matthew 8:17
Psalm 103:2-3 (emphasis added)
Matthew 21:21
Mark 11:23
Luke 10:19
Matthew 18:18

86 Healing from High Blood Pressure

HEAVENLY FATHER, thank You that You are Jehovah Rapha, the God who heals me. Thank You that Jesus bore all my sicknesses, infirmities, and pains upon Himself at the cross, and by His stripes I was healed two thousand years ago. Jesus already paid the price for me to walk in divine health. Healing is part of my inheritance. Healing is my bread. By faith, I receive healing and freedom from high blood pressure and any other sickness or disease in my body, in the name of Jesus.

Father, I repent for all the sins of my ancestors and any dietary or lifestyle habits they had that may have opened the door to a generational curse of hypertension. I break every generational curse and genetic weakness associated with hypertension, heart disease, or any other disease or sickness off me and my descendants, in the mighty name of Jesus. I declare that we have a new bloodline and lineage in Christ Jesus free from hypertension, heart disease, or any other health issues.

Lord, You said in Matthew 21:21 that if I have faith and do not doubt, I can do the same thing You did to the fig tree when You cursed it and it withered and died. You said I can command a mountain to be removed, and if I don't doubt, it will be done. So, I curse hypertension at the root and command it to leave my body and never come back, in Jesus' name. I command my blood pressure to be normal, in the name of Jesus. I cover my heart, circulatory system, and every part of my body with the healing, delivering, restoring blood of the Lord Jesus Christ.

Father, I know that sometimes the miracle is in the instruction. So, I ask You to show me if I need to make any changes to my diet. Your Word says that You reveal deep and hidden things, so I ask You to reveal any hidden causes of this high blood pressure, such as a magnesium deficiency, dehydration, or sleep apnea, and help me to correct them. Thank You that You will heal and deliver me from hypertension forever and that I will live a long, healthy, blessed life. I pray all these things in the matchless name of Jesus, Amen.

SCRIPTURE REFERENCES

Exodus 15:26
Matthew 8:17
2 Corinthians 5:17
Matthew 21:21

87 Healing from Diabetes

HEAVENLY FATHER, I come to You asking for complete healing from diabetes. Thank You that You are my Healer and Deliverer. In Exodus 15:26, You said, "I am the Lord who heals you." You connected Your name and identity with healing. You said, "I will take sickness away from the midst of you." You said Jesus bore my sicknesses and infirmities upon Himself at the cross, and by His stripes I was healed. You said, "Forget not all His benefits: who forgives all your iniquities, who heals *all* your diseases." Thank You that You are a miracle-working, mountain-moving, way-making, promise-keeping God, and nothing is impossible with You. You are bigger, higher, stronger, and greater than diabetes. Diabetes is no match for You! You use doctors and medicine, but You are not limited to them. You alone are my healer, and You can do what doctors and medicine can't do.

Father, I ask You to touch my pancreas, liver, metabolism, and every part of my body with Your supernatural healing power. Cause my pancreas to be healthy, to produce the right amount of insulin, and to operate perfectly the way You designed it. Cause my blood sugar and insulin levels to be normal. Decongest my liver, and reverse any nonalcoholic fatty liver. Help my metabolism to be healthy and metabolize carbohydrates effectively. Restore me to complete health, vim, vigor, vitality, energy, and strength by the shed blood of Jesus and power of the Holy Spirit.

Lord, You said in Matthew 21:21 that if I have faith and do not doubt, I can do the same thing You did to the fig tree when You cursed it and it withered and died. You said that I can command a mountain to be removed, and if I don't doubt, it will be done. So, I curse diabetes at the root and command it to leave my body and never come back, in Jesus' name. I command diabetes, prediabetes, insulin resistance, and metabolic syndrome to be reversed and healed, in the name of Jesus. I command my body to properly and efficiently metabolize carbohydrates and blood glucose, in the name of Jesus. I speak resurrection life, healing, restoration, and wholeness to every organ, gland, tissue, nerve, blood vessel, cell, bone, muscle, ligament, tendon, and every part of my body, in the name of Jesus. I command my insulin and every biochemical in my body to be balanced and at perfect levels, in Jesus' name. I bind, cut off, cancel, and nullify every demonic assignment and attack against my body, in the name of Jesus.

Father, I repent for all the sins of my ancestors and any dietary or lifestyle habits they had that may have opened the door to a generational curse of diabetes. I break every generational curse and genetic weakness associated with diabetes or any other disease or sickness off me and my descendants, in the mighty name of Jesus. I declare that we have a new bloodline and lineage in Christ Jesus free from diabetes or any other health issues.

Father, I know that sometimes the miracle is in the instruction. So, I ask You to show me if I need to make any changes to my diet, lifestyle, exercise, supplements, or any other area that will foster healing in my body. Help me to do my part to take care of my temple as I trust You to do Your part in the supernatural. Thank You that healing is my bread, my inheritance. I receive my complete healing by faith with thanksgiving and declare that I will live the rest of my days in the divine health that Jesus died to give me. I pray all these things in the all-powerful, healing name of Jesus, Amen.

SCRIPTURE REFERENCES

Exodus 15:26
Exodus 23:25
Isaiah 53:4–5
Matthew 8:17

Psalm 103:2–3
(emphasis added)
Matthew 21:21
Mark 11:23

Luke 10:19
Matthew 18:18

88 Healing from Neurological Disorders

HEAVENLY FATHER, I come to You asking for complete healing from [name neurological disorder]. Thank You that You are my Healer and Deliverer. In Exodus 15:26, You said, "I am the Lord who heals you." You connected Your name and identity with healing. You said, "I will take sickness away from the midst of you." You said Jesus bore my sicknesses and infirmities upon Himself at the cross, and by His stripes I was healed. You said, "Forget not all His benefits: who forgives all your iniquities, who heals *all* your diseases." Thank You that You are a miracle-working, mountain-moving, way-making, promise-keeping God, and nothing is impossible with You! You are bigger, higher, stronger, and greater than [name neurological disorder]. [Name neurological disorder] is no match for You! You use doctors and medicine, but You are not limited to them. You alone are my healer, and You can do what doctors and medicine can't do.

Father, I ask You to totally heal and restore my brain, nervous system, cognition, memory, speech, movement, and anything else that needs healing and bless me with a long, healthy, wonderful life in the name of Jesus. Restore me to complete health, vim, vigor, vitality, energy, and strength by the shed blood of Jesus and power of the Holy Spirit.

Lord, You said in Matthew 21:21 that if I have faith and do not doubt, I can do the same thing You did to the fig tree when You cursed it and it withered and died. You said that I can command a mountain to be removed, and if I don't doubt, it will be done. So, I curse [name of neurological disorder] at the root and command it to leave my body and never come back, in Jesus' name. I command healing, restoration, and wholeness to my brain, spinal cord, and nervous system. I command all tau and amyloid proteins and other plaques to be removed from my brain, in the name of Jesus. I command every neuron and synapse in my body to fire perfectly, in the name of Jesus. I command any damage to my brain and nervous system to be reversed and healed, in the name of Jesus. I command all tremors, weakness, stiffness, neuropathy, and pain [name any other symptoms] to leave my body now, in Jesus' mighty name!

Father, You said that death and life are in the power of our tongue. You told Ezekiel to speak to dead, dry bones and they came to life. I speak resurrection power and life over any parts of the brain, nerves, neurons, blood vessels, muscles, ligaments, tendons, or any other body part that was damaged from [name the neurological disorder], in the name of Jesus.

Father, I repent for all the sins of my ancestors and any dietary or lifestyle habits they had that may have opened the door to a generational curse of [name the neurological disorder]. I break every generational curse and genetic weakness associated with [name the neurological disorder] or any other disease or sickness off me and my descendants, in the mighty name of Jesus. I declare that we have a new bloodline and lineage in Christ Jesus free from neurological disorders or any other health issues.

Father, I know that sometimes the miracle is in the instruction. So, I ask You to show me if I need to make any changes to my diet, lifestyle, exercise, supplements, or any other area that will foster healing in my body. Help me to do my part to take care of my temple as I trust You to do Your part in the supernatural. Thank You that healing is my bread, my inheritance. I receive my complete healing by faith with thanksgiving and declare that I will live the rest of my days in the divine health that Jesus died to give me. I pray all these things in the all-powerful, healing name of Jesus, Amen.

SCRIPTURE REFERENCES

Exodus 15:26	Psalm 103:2–3	Luke 10:19
Exodus 23:25	(emphasis added)	Matthew 18:18
Isaiah 53:4–5	Matthew 21:21	Proverbs 18:21
Matthew 8:17	Mark 11:23	Ezekiel 37:4–5

89 Healing from Respiratory Disorders

Heavenly Father, I come to You asking for complete healing from [name respiratory disorder]. Thank You that You are my Healer and Deliverer. In Exodus 15:26, You said, "I am the Lord who heals you." You connected Your name and identity with healing. You said, "I will take sickness away from the midst of you." You said Jesus bore my sicknesses and infirmities upon Himself at the cross and by His stripes I was healed. You said, "Forget not all His benefits: who forgives all your iniquities, who heals *all* your diseases." Thank You that You are a miracle-working, mountain-moving, way-making, promise-keeping God, and nothing is impossible with You. You are bigger, higher, stronger, and greater than [name respiratory disorder]. [Name respiratory disorder] is no match for You! You use doctors and medicine, but You are not limited to them. You alone are my healer, and You can do what doctors and medicine can't do. I ask You to touch every part of my lungs and respiratory system with Your mighty healing power and wipe out [name the respiratory disorder], in the mighty name of Jesus. Restore me completely to health, as You promised.

You said in Matthew 21:21 that if I have faith and do not doubt, I can do the same thing You did to the fig tree when You cursed it and it withered and died. You said that I can command a mountain to be removed, and if I don't doubt, it will be done. So, I curse [name respiratory disorder] at the root and command it to leave my body and never come back, in Jesus' name. I speak healing, wholeness, and restoration over my lungs and respiratory system and command them to function perfectly the way God designed them, in Jesus' name. I cover my lungs, bronchi, bronchioles, alveoli, and every part of my respiratory system with the healing, delivering, restoring blood of the Lord Jesus Christ.

Father, I repent for all the sins of my ancestors and any dietary or lifestyle habits they had that may have opened the door to a generational curse of [name the respiratory disorder]. I break every generational curse and genetic weakness associated with [name the respiratory disorder] or any other disease or sickness off me and my descendants, in the mighty name of Jesus. I declare that we have a new bloodline and lineage in Christ Jesus free from respiratory disorders or any other health issues.

Father, I know that sometimes the miracle is in the instruction. So, I ask You to show me if I need to make any changes to my diet, lifestyle, exercise, supplements, or any other area that will foster healing in my body. Help me to do my part to take care of my temple as I trust You to do Your part in the supernatural. Thank You that healing is my bread, my inheritance. I receive my complete healing by faith with thanksgiving and declare that I will live the rest of my days in the divine health that Jesus died to give me. I pray all these things in the all-powerful, healing name of Jesus, Amen.

SCRIPTURE REFERENCES

Exodus 15:26
Isaiah 53:4–5
Matthew 8:17
1 Peter 2:24
Psalm 103:2–3
Exodus 23:25
Matthew 21:21

---

90 Healing from GI Disorders

HEAVENLY FATHER, I come to You asking for complete healing from gastrointestinal issues [name the specific disorder if you know it]. Thank You that You are my Healer and Deliverer. In Exodus 15:26, You said, "I am the Lord who heals you." You connected Your name and identity with healing. You said, "I will take sickness away from the midst of you." You said Jesus bore my sicknesses and infirmities upon Himself at the cross and by His stripes I was healed. Thank You that You are a miracle-working, mountain-moving, way-making, promise-keeping God, and nothing is impossible with You! So, I ask You to completely heal my entire GI tract. Wipe out [name the specific disorder if you know it], every disease, disorder, dysfunction, and symptom in my GI tract and cause it to function perfectly the way You designed it to. Restore my GI tract and body to complete health, harmony, and balance, in the mighty name of Jesus.

Father, You said that life and death are in the power of the tongue. When Jesus cursed the fig tree and it withered and died, He told His disciples, "Assuredly, I say to you, if you have faith and do not doubt, you will not only do what was done to the fig tree, but also if you say to this mountain, 'Be removed and be cast into the sea,' it will be done." Jesus also said in Mark 11:23 that if I don't doubt in my heart, I can have whatever things I say. So, I curse every GI disorder [name the specific disorder if you know it] at the root and command it to wither and die, bear no more fruit, and leave my body, in the mighty name of Jesus. I cover my GI tract, gut microbiome, and every organ, gland, tissue, and cell in my body with the healing, delivering, restoring blood of Jesus. I speak healing, wholeness, restoration, and shalom peace over my GI tract and body, in Jesus' name. I declare that I am healed by the stripes of Jesus. No weapon formed against me shall prosper.

Father, I know that You can use doctors and medical professionals to facilitate healing. So, I ask You to give my medical care team wisdom and anointing to treat me in the most effective way. I also know that sometimes the miracle is in the instruction. So, help me to tune my spiritual ears to hear any divine instruction You want to give me about changes I need to make in my diet, lifestyle, or anything else that would help my body heal. Thank You for healing me and that I will live out the rest of my days in divine health, vim, vigor, vitality, energy, and strength by the shed blood of Jesus and the power of the Holy Spirit. Healing is my inheritance, and I receive it by faith with thanksgiving. I pray all these things in the healing, delivering, restoring name of Jesus, Amen.

SCRIPTURE REFERENCES

Exodus 15:26	Matthew 8:17	Matthew 21:21
Exodus 23:25	1 Peter 2:24	Mark 11:23
Isaiah 53:4–5	Proverbs 18:21	Isaiah 54:17

---

91 Healing from Pain

HEAVENLY FATHER, thank You that You are Jehovah Rapha, the God who heals me. Thank You that Jesus "bore our sicknesses, and he carried our pains [on the cross] . . . and we are healed by his wounds." Lord, according to this promise, I ask You to remove all sickness and pain from my body. I ask You to lay an axe to the root cause of this pain and restore me completely to health. Thank You that according to Psalm 103:3, You heal all my diseases, and according to Exodus 23:25, You remove all sickness from me.

Lord, after You cursed the fig tree and it withered and died, You said in Matthew 21:21, "Assuredly, I say to you, if you have faith and do not doubt, you will not only do what was done to the fig tree, but also if you say to this mountain, 'Be removed and be cast into the sea,' it will be done." So, I curse this pain in my body at the root and command pain and whatever is causing it [name it if you know the cause] to wither and die and bear no more fruit, in the mighty name of Jesus. Sickness and pain, I command you to leave my body and never come back, in Jesus' name. I speak healing, wholeness, and restoration over every organ, gland, tissue, bone, muscle, ligament, tendon, cell, and every part of my body, in the name of Jesus. I cover every part of my body with the healing, delivering, restoring blood of the Lord Jesus Christ.

Father, thank You for healing me and that I will live out all my days in the divine health and freedom from pain that Jesus died to give me. I receive it by faith. In Jesus' precious name, Amen.

SCRIPTURE REFERENCES

Exodus 15:26
Isaiah 53:4–5 [CSB]
Matthew 8:17
1 Peter 2:24
Psalm 103:3
Exodus 23:25
Matthew 21:21

92 Healing from Female Problems

HEAVENLY FATHER, I come to You asking for complete healing from female-related problems [name the specific disorder if you know it]. Thank You that You are my Healer and Deliverer. In Exodus 15:26, You said, "I am the Lord who heals you." You connected Your name and identity with healing. You said, "I will take sickness away from the midst of you." You said Jesus bore my sicknesses and infirmities upon Himself at the cross and by His stripes I was healed. Thank You that You are a miracle-working, mountain-moving, way-making, promise-keeping God, and nothing is impossible with You. I ask You to completely heal me from all female-related health problems [name the specific disorder if you know it]. Wipe out every sickness, disease, disorder, and symptom from my body, and cause it to function perfectly the way You designed it to. Cause all my hormones and biochemicals to be at optimal levels. Restore my body to perfect health, harmony, and balance, in the mighty name of Jesus.

Father, You said that life and death are in the power of the tongue. When Jesus cursed the fig tree and it withered and died, He told His disciples, "Assuredly, I say to you, if you have faith and do not doubt, you will not only do what was done to the fig tree, but also if you say to this mountain, 'Be removed and be cast into the sea,' it will be done." Jesus also said in Mark 11:23 that if I don't doubt in my heart, I can have whatever things I say. So, I curse [name the specific disorder] at the root and command it to wither and die, bear no more fruit, and leave my body, in the mighty name of Jesus. I cover every organ, gland, tissue, cell, blood, bone, muscle, ligament, tendon, and every part of my body with the healing, delivering, restoring blood of Jesus. I speak healing, wholeness, restoration, and shalom peace over every part of my body, in Jesus' name. I declare that I am healed by the stripes of Jesus. No weapon formed against me shall prosper.

Father, I know that You can use doctors and medical professionals to facilitate healing. So, I ask You to give my medical care team wisdom and anointing to treat me in the most effective way. I also know that sometimes the miracle is in the instruction. So, help me to tune my spiritual ears to hear any divine instruction You want to give me about changes to diet and lifestyle, supplements, exercise, or anything else that would help my body heal. Thank You for healing me and that I will live out the rest of my days in divine health, vim, vigor, vitality, energy, and strength by the shed blood of Jesus and the power of the Holy Spirit. Healing is my inheritance, and I receive it by faith with thanksgiving. I pray all these things in the healing, delivering, restoring name of Jesus, Amen.

SCRIPTURE REFERENCES

Exodus 15:26	Matthew 8:17	Matthew 21:21
Exodus 23:25	1 Peter 2:24	Mark 11:23
Isaiah 53:4–5	Proverbs 18:21	Isaiah 54:17

93 Healing from Male Problems

HEAVENLY FATHER, I come to You asking for complete healing from male-related problems [name the specific disorder if you know it]. Thank You that You are my Healer and Deliverer. In Exodus 15:26, You said, "I am the Lord who heals you." You connected Your name and identity with healing. You said, "I will take sickness away from the midst of you." You said Jesus bore my sicknesses and infirmities upon Himself at the cross and by His stripes I was healed. Thank You that You are a miracle-working, mountain-moving, way-making, promise-keeping God, and nothing is impossible with You! I ask You to completely heal me from all male-related health problems [name the specific disorder if you know it]. Wipe out every sickness, disease, disorder, and symptom from my body, and cause it to function perfectly the way You designed it to. Restore my body to perfect health, harmony, and balance, in the mighty name of Jesus.

Father, You said that life and death are in the power of the tongue. When Jesus cursed the fig tree and it withered and died, He told His disciples, "Assuredly, I say to you, if you have faith and do not doubt, you will not only do what was done to the fig tree, but also if you say to this mountain, 'Be removed and be cast into the sea,' it will be done." Jesus also said in Mark 11:23 that if I don't doubt in my heart, I can have whatever things I say. So, I curse [name the specific disorder] at the root and command it to wither and die, bear no more fruit, and leave my body, in the mighty name of Jesus. I cover every organ, gland, tissue, cell, blood, bone, muscle, ligament, tendon, and every part of my body with the healing, delivering, restoring blood of Jesus. I speak healing, wholeness, restoration, and shalom peace over every part of my body, in Jesus' name. I declare that I am healed by the stripes of Jesus. No weapon formed against me shall prosper.

Father, I know that You can use doctors and medical professionals to facilitate healing. So, I ask You to give my medical care team wisdom and anointing to treat me in the most effective way. I also know that sometimes the miracle is in the instruction. So, help me to tune my spiritual ears to hear any divine instruction You want to give me about changes to diet and lifestyle, supplements, exercise, or anything else that would help my body heal. Thank You for healing me and that I will live out the rest of my days in divine health, vim, vigor, vitality, energy, and strength by the shed blood of Jesus and the power of the Holy Spirit. Healing is my inheritance, and I receive it by faith with thanksgiving. I pray all these things in the healing, delivering, restoring name of Jesus, Amen.

SCRIPTURE REFERENCES

Exodus 15:26	Matthew 8:17	Matthew 21:21
Exodus 23:25	1 Peter 2:24	Mark 11:23
Isaiah 53:4–5	Proverbs 18:21	Isaiah 54:17

94 Healing from Infertility

HEAVENLY FATHER, I come to You asking for complete healing from infertility. One of the first things You said after You created man was, "Be fruitful and multiply." Your Word says, "Children are a gift from the Lord; they are a reward from him." Father, You healed Sarah, Rebekah, Rachel, Hannah, and the Shunammite woman from infertility in the Bible. So, I ask You to heal my body of any infertility issues [name any specific disorder if you know it]. Thank You that You are my Healer and Deliverer. In Exodus 15:26, You said, "I am the Lord who heals you." You connected Your name and identity with healing. You said, "I will take sickness away from the midst of you." You said Jesus bore my sicknesses and infirmities upon Himself at the cross and by His stripes I was healed. Thank You that You are a miracle-working, mountain-moving, way-making, promise-keeping God, and nothing is impossible with You! So, I ask You to completely heal me. Wipe out any fertility issues in my body and cause my body to function perfectly the way You designed it to, in the mighty name of Jesus.

Father, I ask You to touch every part of my body related to fertility, including my hormones, with Your *dunamis*, miracle-working, healing power and restore my body to complete health. You said that life and death are in the power of the tongue. Jesus said, "Assuredly, I say to you, whoever says to this mountain, 'Be removed and be cast into the sea,' and does not doubt in his heart, but believes that those things he says will be done, he will have whatever he says." So, I speak to the mountain of infertility and command it to leave my body, in the mighty name of Jesus. I speak healing, wholeness, and restoration over every part of my body, in Jesus' name. I declare that I am healed by the stripes of Jesus. No weapon formed against me shall prosper. I will have as many children as I desire to have.

Father, I know that You can use doctors and medical professionals to facilitate healing. So, I ask You to give my medical care team wisdom and anointing to treat me in the most effective way. I also know that sometimes the miracle is in the instruction. So, help me to tune my spiritual ears to hear any divine instruction You want to give me about changes to my diet, lifestyle, supplements, exercise, or anything else that would help my body heal. Thank You for healing me and that I will live out the rest of my days in divine health, vim, vigor, vitality, energy, and strength by the shed blood of Jesus and the power of the Holy Spirit. Healing is my inheritance, and I receive it by faith with thanksgiving. I pray all these things in the healing, delivering, restoring name of Jesus, Amen.

> **SCRIPTURE REFERENCES**
>
> Genesis 1:28
> Psalm 127:3 NLT
> Exodus 15:26
> Exodus 23:25
>
> Isaiah 53:4–5
> Matthew 8:17
> 1 Peter 2:24
> Proverbs 18:21
>
> Mark 11:23
> Isaiah 54:17

95 Healing from Stroke

HEAVENLY FATHER, I come to You asking for complete healing from stroke. Thank You that You are my Healer and Deliverer. In Exodus 15:26, You said, "I am the Lord who heals you." You connected Your name and identity with healing. You said, "I will take sickness away from the midst of you." You said Jesus bore my sicknesses and infirmities upon Himself at the cross and by His stripes I was healed. Thank You that You are a miracle-working, mountain-moving, way-making, promise-keeping God, and nothing is impossible with You. Romans 8:11 says the same Spirit who raised Jesus from the dead dwells in me and gives life, energy, and strength to my mortal body. So, I ask the Holy Spirit to touch every organ, brain cell, tissue, nerve, neuron, synapse, muscle, ligament, tendon, and every part of my body with Your miracle-working, resurrection, healing power. Reverse every effect from this stroke. Restore my cognition, memory, speech, and movement completely, in the mighty name of Jesus.

Father, You said that life and death are in the power of the tongue. You told Ezekiel to speak to dead, dry bones, and they came to life. So, I speak healing, wholeness, restoration, and resurrection over my brain, nervous system, circulatory system, muscles, ligaments, tendons, and every part of my body, in the mighty name of Jesus. I command dead brain cells, nerves, and tissues to come back to life, in Jesus' mighty name. Lord, You healed paralytics when You walked the earth, and Hebrews 13:8 says You are the same yesterday, today, and forever. So, I ask You to heal and reverse all paralysis in my body. I declare that I am healed by the stripes of Jesus. No weapon formed against me shall prosper.

Father, I know that You can use doctors and medical professionals to facilitate healing. So, I ask You to give my medical care team wisdom and anointing to treat me in the most effective way. I also know that sometimes the miracle is in the instruction. So, help me to tune my spiritual ears to hear any divine instruction You want to give me about changes I need to make in my diet, lifestyle, or anything else that would help my body heal. Thank You for healing me and that I will live out the rest of my days in divine health, vim, vigor, vitality, energy, and strength by the shed blood of Jesus and the power of the Holy Spirit. Healing is my inheritance, and I receive it by faith with thanksgiving. I pray all these things in the healing, delivering, restoring name of Jesus, Amen.

SCRIPTURE REFERENCES

Exodus 15:26
Exodus 23:25
Isaiah 53:4–5
Matthew 8:17
1 Peter 2:24
Proverbs 18:21
Ezekiel 37:4–5
Hebrews 13:8
Isaiah 54:17
Matthew 21:21
Mark 11:23

96 Healing from Eye, Sight Problems

HEAVENLY FATHER, I come to You asking for complete healing from every problem with my eyes [name the specific disorder if you know it]. Thank You that You are my Healer and Deliverer. In Exodus 15:26, You said, "I am the Lord who heals you." You connected Your name and identity with healing. You said, "I will take sickness away from the midst of you." You said Jesus bore my sicknesses and infirmities upon Himself at the cross and by His stripes I was healed. Thank You that You are a miracle-working, mountain-moving, way-making, promise-keeping God, and nothing is impossible with You. I ask You to completely heal my eyes and sight. Wipe out [name the specific disorder if you know it], every disease, disorder, infection, and symptom in my eyes, and cause them to function perfectly the way You designed them to. Restore my eyes, sight, and body to complete health, in the mighty name of Jesus.

Father, You said that life and death are in the power of the tongue. When Jesus cursed the fig tree and it withered and died, He told His disciples, "Assuredly, I say to you, if you have faith and do not doubt, you will not only do what was done to the fig tree, but also if you say to this mountain, 'Be removed and be cast into the sea,' it will be done." Jesus also said in Mark 11:23 that if I don't doubt in my heart, I can have whatever things I say. So, I curse every eye disorder [name the specific disorder if you know it] at the root and command it to wither and die, bear no more fruit, and leave my body, in the mighty name of Jesus. I cover every part of my eyes with the healing, delivering, sanctifying blood of Jesus. I speak healing, wholeness, restoration, and shalom peace over my eyes and body, in Jesus' name. I declare that I am healed by the stripes of Jesus. No weapon formed against me shall prosper.

Father, I know that You can use doctors and medical professionals to facilitate healing. So, I ask You to give my medical care team wisdom and anointing to treat me in the most effective way. I also know that sometimes the miracle is in the instruction. So, help me to tune my spiritual ears to hear any divine instruction You want to give me about changes I need to make in my diet, lifestyle, supplements, exercise, or anything else that would help my body heal. Thank You for healing me and that I will live out the rest of my days in divine health, vim, vigor, vitality, energy, and strength by the shed blood of Jesus and the power of the Holy Spirit. Healing is my inheritance, and I receive it by faith with thanksgiving. I pray all these things in the healing, delivering, restoring name of Jesus, Amen.

SCRIPTURE REFERENCES

Exodus 15:26	Matthew 8:17	Matthew 21:21
Exodus 23:25	1 Peter 2:24	Mark 11:23
Isaiah 53:4–5	Proverbs 18:21	Isaiah 54:17

97 Healing from Ear, Hearing Problems

HEAVENLY FATHER, I come to You asking for complete healing from every problem with my ears [name the specific disorder if you know it]. Thank You that You are my Healer and Deliverer. In Exodus 15:26, You said, "I am the Lord who heals you." You connected Your name and identity with healing. You said, "I will take sickness away from the midst of you." You said Jesus bore my sicknesses and infirmities upon Himself at the cross and by His stripes I was healed. Thank You that You are a miracle-working, mountain-moving, way-making, promise-keeping God, and nothing is impossible with You. I ask You to completely heal my ears and hearing. Wipe out [name the specific disorder if you know it], every disease, disorder, infection, and symptom in my ears, and cause them to function perfectly the way You designed them. Restore my ears, hearing, and body to complete health, in the mighty name of Jesus.

Father, You said that life and death are in the power of the tongue. When Jesus cursed the fig tree and it withered and died, He told His disciples, "Assuredly, I say to you, if you have faith and do not doubt, you will not only do what was done to the fig tree, but also if you say to this mountain, 'Be removed and be cast into the sea,' it will be done." Jesus also said in Mark 11:23 that if I don't doubt in my heart, I can have whatever things I say. So, I curse every ear disorder [name the specific disorder if you know it] at the root and command it to wither and die, bear no more fruit, and leave my body, in the mighty name of Jesus. I cover every part of my ears with the healing, delivering, sanctifying blood of Jesus. I speak healing, wholeness, restoration, and shalom peace over my ears and body, in Jesus' name. I declare that I am healed by the stripes of Jesus. No weapon formed against me shall prosper.

Father, I know that You can use doctors and medical professionals to facilitate healing. So, I ask You to give my medical care team wisdom and anointing to treat me in the most effective way. I also know that sometimes the miracle is in the instruction. So, help me to tune my spiritual ears to hear any divine instruction You want to give me about changes I need to make in my diet, lifestyle, supplements, exercise, or anything else that would help my body heal. Thank You for healing me and that I will live out the rest of my days in divine health, vim, vigor, vitality, energy, and strength by the shed blood of Jesus and the power of the Holy Spirit. Healing is my inheritance, and I receive it by faith with thanksgiving. I pray all these things in the healing, delivering, restoring name of Jesus, Amen.

SCRIPTURE REFERENCES

Exodus 15:26	Matthew 8:17	Matthew 21:21
Exodus 23:25	1 Peter 2:24	Mark 11:23
Isaiah 53:4–5	Proverbs 18:21	Isaiah 54:17

98 Prayer for Wisdom in Health-Care Decisions

HEAVENLY FATHER, I come to You seeking wisdom in my health-care decisions. I want to be Spirit-led and make the best decisions that will facilitate my healing. You said, "If any of you lacks wisdom, let him ask of God, who gives to all liberally and without reproach, and it will be given to him." So, I ask You to give me wisdom liberally. Thank You that Your Spirit who lives inside of me is called the Spirit of wisdom, understanding, knowledge, and counsel and that I have access to His wisdom at all times. You said, "As many as are led by the Spirit of God, these are sons of God." Help me to be sensitive to the Holy Spirit's gentle promptings and still, small voice and be led by Him in every decision I make. Help me to trust and obey His leading, even if it contradicts my doctor or conventional wisdom. Your thoughts are not our thoughts, and Your ways are not our ways. You know what is best for me.

Father, I know that You can use doctors and medical professionals to facilitate healing. So, I ask You to give my medical care team wisdom and anointing to treat me in the most effective way. I also know that sometimes the miracle is in the instruction. You said, "I will instruct you and teach you in the way you should go; I will counsel you with my loving eye on you." Help me to tune my spiritual ears to hear any divine instruction and guidance You have about my diet, lifestyle, supplements, exercise, alternative treatments, or anything else that would help my body heal. Thank You that Your wisdom and guidance will help me to reclaim the divine health Jesus died to give me. Healing is my bread, my inheritance, and I receive it by faith with thanksgiving. I pray all these things in the healing, delivering, restoring name of Jesus, Amen.

SCRIPTURE REFERENCES
James 1:5
Romans 8:14
Isaiah 55:8
Psalm 32:8 NIV

99 Prayer Before a Medical Test

HEAVENLY FATHER, I lift up my upcoming [name the test, MRI, scan, etc.]. Thank You that You have me in the palm of Your hand. You are Jehovah Rapha, the God who heals me, and You are going to use this [name the test, MRI, scan, etc.] to help my doctor(s) make the best decisions about my treatment and facilitate healing in my body.

Father, I ask You to bless this [name the test, MRI, scan, etc.] and that it would go smoothly and easily. Remove all fear and anxiety from me about the actual [name the test, MRI, scan, etc.] or the results. Fill me with Your shalom peace that surpasses all understanding, and help me to rest in the knowledge that You are on the throne and in control.

Father, You said, "Whatever things you ask when you pray, believe that you receive them." You also said, "Ask, and *it will* be given to you." So, I ask that You completely heal me and that the result of this [name the test, MRI, scan, etc.] would show that nothing is wrong with my body. I pray for a supernaturally favorable result that is exceedingly, abundantly above all I could ask or think.

Father, Thank You that according to Psalm 138:8, You are perfecting everything that concerns me, including this [name the test, MRI, scan, etc.]. You said that in all things I am more than a conqueror and that You always lead me to triumph in Christ Jesus. Thank You that You are going to bring me out of this health challenge with the victory. I pray all these things in Jesus' precious name, Amen.

SCRIPTURE REFERENCES

Exodus 15:26
Ephesians 3:20
2 Corinthians 2:14
Luke 11:9 (emphasis added)
Philippians 4:7
Mark 11:24
Psalm 138:8
Romans 8:37

100 Prayer Before a Medical Procedure

HEAVENLY FATHER, I lift up this [name the medical procedure] I am having. Thank You that You have me in the palm of Your hand. Thank You that You have given Your angels charge over me to keep me in all my ways and bear me up in their hands. You are Jehovah Rapha, the God who heals me, and You are going to use this procedure to foster healing in my body.

Father, I ask for Your blessings upon this procedure. Anoint the minds and hands of the doctor(s), nurses, and everyone participating in this procedure. I pray that it will go smoothly and flawlessly, with no adverse reactions or complications, and that I will recover quickly.

I cover me, the procedure, and everyone involved with the blood of Jesus. Surround me with Your hedge of protection and mighty angels on all sides. I bind any forces of darkness that would try to interfere with this procedure in any way, in Jesus' name.

Father, fill me with Your shalom peace that surpasses all understanding. Remove all fear and anxiety from me, and help me to rest in the knowledge that You are on the throne and in control. Thank You that according to Psalm 138:8, You are perfecting everything that concerns me, including this procedure. You said that in all things I am more than a conqueror and that You always lead me to triumph in Christ Jesus. Thank You that You are going to bring me out of this health challenge with the victory. I pray all these things in Jesus' precious name, Amen.

SCRIPTURE REFERENCES

Psalm 91:11–12
Exodus 15:26
Job 1:10
Romans 8:37
2 Corinthians 2:14
Psalm 138:8

101 Prayer for Doctors, Nurses, Other Care Providers

FATHER GOD, thank You for every doctor, nurse, health-care worker, social worker, chaplain, pastor, and everyone else involved in my care. I ask You to give them Your supernatural wisdom, guidance, and anointing so that they can give me and others the best care possible. [If you need surgery] Father, I ask You to guide the surgeon's hands. Anoint him/her and all those assisting in the surgery and help them to perform the surgery flawlessly.

When they are feeling weary and need encouragement, pour Your grace upon them and send angels to minister to them. Strengthen their bodies and minds. Bless them in every area of their lives, keep them healthy, provide for all their needs, and protect them and their families.

I pray that if any of them do not know Jesus as their Lord and Savior, You would reveal Yourself to them and they would receive salvation in Christ. Help me to be a good witness to them and be bold about sharing my faith when You prompt me to. In Jesus' precious name I pray, Amen.

SCRIPTURE REFERENCES
Luke 11:9

102 Prayer for Another Person's Healing

HEAVENLY FATHER, thank You that [person's name] is Your precious child. You love him/her with an unfailing, everlasting love. You have him/her in the palm of Your hand. You are his/her Healer and Deliverer. You are a miracle-working, way-making, promise-keeping God and nothing is too hard for You. I ask You to touch [person's name] from the top of his/her head to the bottom of his/her feet with Your mighty healing power. Wipe out every trace of sickness and disease [name anything specific—cancer, infection, etc.] from his/her body and restore him/her completely to health.

Thank You that Jesus already bore [person's name's] sickness, infirmities, and pains upon Himself at the cross and by His stripes he/she is healed. No weapon formed against him/her shall prosper. With long life, You will satisfy him/her and show him/her Your salvation. He/she will live and not die to declare the works of the Lord.

Father, Your Word says that death and life are in the power of my tongue. You said in Matthew 21:21 that if I have faith and do not doubt, I can do the same thing You did to the fig tree when You cursed it and it withered and died. You said I can command a mountain to be removed and if I don't doubt, it will be done. So, I curse every sickness, infirmity, and infection in [name's] body and command it to wither and die and leave his/her body, in the name of Jesus. I speak healing, wholeness, and restoration over every organ, gland, tissue, cell, bone, muscle, tendon, ligament, and his/her blood, in the name of Jesus.

Father, You said, "The prayer of faith will save the sick, and the Lord will raise him up." Thank You for hearing my prayer of faith and completely healing [person's name]. I pray all these things in the healing, delivering name of Jesus, Amen.

SCRIPTURE REFERENCES

Exodus 15:26	Psalm 91:16	Matthew 8:17
Isaiah 53:4-5	Psalm 118:17	1 Peter 2:24
Isaiah 54:17	Proverbs 18:21	James 5:15

VII
HEALING THE SOUL

103 General Prayer for Healing the Soul

HEAVENLY FATHER, I come to You for healing in my soul. You are Jehovah Rapha, the God who heals me. You heal not only my physical body but also my soul. Psalm 23:3 says that You restore my soul. Your Holy Spirit who lives inside of me can touch me in the depths of my soul where no person can touch and completely heal and restore my soul. I give You full access to every hurt pocket in my soul and ask You to put Your healing balm upon every bad memory from the past, every trauma, abuse, betrayal, rejection, mistreatment, loss, pain, mistake, failure, negative words people have spoken over me, and everything else in my soul that is not from You. Heal, deliver, restore, and make me whole in my soul. You said, "Beloved, I pray that you may prosper in all things and be in health, just as your soul prospers." Cause my soul to be healthy and prosper so that I can become all You created me to be and live my best life.

Father, I know that freedom begins with repentance, so I repent for every lie I have believed. I repent for holding on to any unforgiveness, offense, bitterness, anger, self-pity, negativity, low self-esteem, and every other kind of unhealthiness or dysfunction in my soul. I ask You to forgive me, wash me clean by the blood of Jesus, and close every door to the enemy. The apostle Paul wrote, "Forgetting what lies behind and straining forward to what lies ahead, I press on toward the goal for the prize of the upward call of God in Christ Jesus." Help me to forget the past so that I can press on and lay hold of all that You have in store for my future.

Your Word says that You are the Potter, and we are the clay. You can take our marred places and fashion us into a beautiful new vessel. I ask that You heal the marred, broken places in my soul and mold me into a healthy, beautiful vessel for Your glory. You said, "If anyone is in Christ, he is a new creation; old things have passed away; behold, all things have become new." I pray that all the negative experiences and soul wounds from the past would pass away and I would become that new creation in Christ.

Lord, You commanded me to forgive others just as You have forgiven me in Christ Jesus. Help me to truly forgive everyone who has ever wronged me. Help me to release them and the pain they caused to You so that I can be healed and free in my soul. Thank You that I am moving forward with a healthy soul and will enjoy the abundant life that Jesus died to give me. I will have healthy, peaceful relationships. I will reach my full potential and fulfill every plan and purpose You have for my life. I pray all these things in Jesus' precious name, Amen.

SCRIPTURE REFERENCES

Exodus 15:16 Philippians 3:13–14 ESV Ephesians 4:32
Psalm 23:3 Jeremiah 18:3–6
3 John 2 2 Corinthians 5:17

104 Prayer of Forgiveness

HEAVENLY FATHER, Your Word commands us to forgive others just as You have forgiven us in Christ Jesus. Jesus said if we don't forgive others their trespasses, You won't forgive our trespasses.

Help me to understand that holding onto unforgiveness only hurts me. I repent for harboring unforgiveness, bitterness, offense, and anger toward anyone. I ask You to forgive me and cleanse my soul of all unforgiveness and every ungodly emotion associated with it. I choose as an act of obedience to forgive every person who has hurt, wronged, offended, rejected, and betrayed me. I specifically forgive [name out loud specific people]. I let them off the hook for what they did to me. I release them and the pain they caused me. You said, "Vengeance is Mine, I will repay," so I trust You to deal with them and repay me for the wrong they did.

Your Word says that even unbelievers love those who are good to them. But You called us to a higher standard and commanded us to love even our enemies and to pray for and bless those who have wronged us. You said when we do that, our reward will be great. Help me not only to forgive but to love and pray for those who hurt me. Empower me to walk in Your love, which keeps no record of wrongs, bears all things, endures all things, and never fails.

I also choose to forgive myself for every mistake, failure, and sin I have committed. Your Word says that You have not only forgiven me, but You have separated my sins from me as far as the east is from the west and remember them no more. Help me to forgive myself and let go of all guilt, shame, and condemnation so that I can be free to become all You created me to be and embrace the new things You have for me. I pray all these things in the healing, delivering, restoring name of the Lord Jesus Christ, Amen.

SCRIPTURE REFERENCES

Ephesians 4:32
Matthew 6:14-15
Hebrews 10:30
Luke 6:32-36
Matthew 5:44
1 Corinthians 13:4-8
Psalm 103:12
Psalm 23:3

105 Healing from Abandonment

HEAVENLY FATHER, I come to You needing healing from the pain and scars of abandonment. Your Word says that You restore my soul and heal the brokenhearted and bind up their wounds. I ask You to heal my heart, bind up my wounds, and restore my soul. Wash away the pain and every remnant of abandonment in my soul. Thank You that even though [name the person—my father, mother, parents, husband, etc.] abandoned me, You will never leave me nor forsake me. Jesus said, "I am with you always, even to the end of the age." Psalm 27:10 says, "Even if my father and mother abandon me, the Lord will hold me close." Thank You that I can always count on Your unfailing love and abiding presence in my life.

Thank You that I am not defined by what other people did to me or by my past. I am only defined by what You say about me. You say that I am a child of God, fearfully and wonderfully made, a masterpiece handcrafted by You, so worthy of love that You sent Your only Son to die for me, a new creation in Christ, and totally accepted and approved by You. Help me not to believe the lies of the enemy that I am unlovable, that it was my fault, that people can't be trusted, or that it will happen again. The apostle Paul wrote, "One thing I do: forgetting what lies behind and straining forward to what lies ahead, I press on." Help me to let go of the past and press on to lay hold of the wonderful things You have in my future.

Help me to forgive and release the person/people who abandoned me. Deliver me from the suspicion and fear that other people may abandon me. Heal me so completely that I can love as if I've never been hurt and have healthy, rich relationships. I ask You to bring the right people into my life, who will not abandon or hurt me, and keep the wrong people out of my life. I bind, rebuke, cut off, and cast out any spirit of abandonment, fear, distrust, insecurity, or any other spirit that gained access to me through abandonment, in the name of Jesus. Instead, I have received the Spirit of adoption by whom I cry "Abba, Father." By faith, I receive complete healing, wholeness, and freedom from abandonment. I will walk in confident assurance that I am unconditionally loved, accepted, and approved and that my best days are ahead of me. I pray all these things in Jesus' precious name, Amen.

SCRIPTURE REFERENCES

Psalm 23:3	Matthew 28:20	Romans 8:15
Psalm 147:3	Psalm 27:10 NLT	
Hebrews 13:5	Philippians 3:13–14 ESV	

106 Healing After Abortion

HEAVENLY FATHER, I approach Your throne of mercy and grace to repent for having an abortion, and I ask for Your forgiveness. Thank You that Your love, grace, and mercy are greater than my sins. Thank You that the blood of Jesus washed away all my sins and there is "no condemnation for those who are in Christ Jesus." Jesus took every charge against me and nailed it to the cross, canceling every record of wrong against me. You have removed my sins from me as far as the east is from the west, and You remember them no more. Though my sins are like scarlet, You made them white as snow. Father, help me to receive Your forgiveness and mercy. Help me to forgive myself and not continue beating myself up and listening to the accuser of the brethren, because You have already forgiven me. Help me to let go of that mistake because You are not holding it against me. Your Word says You've chosen not to remember it.

Father, remind me that great heroes of the Bible made terrible mistakes. Your Word says, "All have sinned and fall short of the glory of God." Moses killed an Egyptian. David committed adultery with Bathsheba and had her husband killed. Peter publicly denied Jesus three times. Paul imprisoned Christians and approved of Stephen being stoned to death. Yet You forgave them and used them in even greater ways after their mistakes. You are a God of mercy and the second chance. When everyone wanted to stone the woman caught in the act of adultery, Jesus helped her up and said, "Neither do I condemn you; go and sin no more." He offered salvation to the woman at the well who had five previous husbands and was living with a man who wasn't her husband. Father, help me to understand that I am not defined by my past sins and mistakes. You forgave these people and gave them a new beginning, and You will do the same for me. You said, "Forget the former things; do not dwell on the past. See, I am doing a new thing!" The apostle Paul said, "Forgetting those things which are behind and reaching forward to those things which are ahead, I press toward the . . . upward call of God in Christ Jesus." Help me to let go of the past and embrace the wonderful things You have in my future.

Father, Your Word says that You restore my soul. I ask You to heal and restore my soul from the pain of that mistake. Put Your healing balm on my soul and wash away all guilt, shame, condemnation, and pain. Help me to be free and healthy in my soul. Restore my joy and peace. Thank You that You give me "beauty for ashes, the oil of joy for mourning, the garment of praise for the spirit of heaviness." I bind, rebuke, cut off, and cast out every spirit of shame, guilt, condemnation, accusation, blame, regret, depression, lies, and every demonic spirit from me, in the name of Jesus. I declare that I am forgiven, free, and victorious in Christ. I let go of the past and reach forward to great things God has in store for me. It's in Jesus' precious name I pray, Amen.

SCRIPTURE REFERENCES

Romans 8:1 NIV
Colossians 2:14
Psalm 103:12
Hebrews 8:12

Isaiah 1:18 NLT
Romans 3:23
John 8:11
John 4:7–26

Isaiah 43:18–19
Philippians 3:13–14
Psalm 23:3
Isaiah 61:3

107 Healing from Abuse

Heavenly Father, I come to You needing healing from the pain and scars of abuse. I ask You to heal my heart, bind up my wounds, and restore my soul. Wash away the pain and every remnant of abuse by the blood of Jesus, and close every door to the enemy. Thank You that You are the healer and restorer of my soul. You redeem my life from destruction and give me beauty for ashes. You take what the enemy meant for evil and turn it for good. Help me to forgive [name the person/people who abused you], as You commanded me to do. By Your grace, enable me to truly release them and the pain they caused me. Set me free from all grief, anger, bitterness, hatred, resentment, depression, self-esteem and identity issues, and every effect of abuse.

Thank You that I am not defined by what other people did to me or my past. I am only defined by what You say about me. You say that I am a child of God, fearfully and wonderfully made, a masterpiece handcrafted by You, so worthy of love that You sent Your only Son to die for me, a new creation in Christ, and totally accepted and approved by You. Help me to reject any lies or wrong beliefs from things people did or said to me in the past. Your Word says that You are the Potter and we are the clay. You can take our marred places and fashion us into a beautiful new vessel. I ask that You heal the marred, broken places in my soul and mold me into a healthy, beautiful vessel for Your glory. You said, "If any man be in Christ, he is a new creation; old things have passed away; all things have become new." I pray that every abuse, painful memory, and soul wound from the past would pass away, and I would become that new, free, victorious creation in Christ.

Psalm 23:3 says, "He restores my soul." Father, I ask You to completely heal and restore my soul. Restore my self-esteem. Restore my identity in Christ. Restore my peace and joy. Restore everything the enemy damaged or stole from me through abuse. I reject every lie of the enemy that I am damaged goods, unlovable, that I'll never recover, or [name any other lies the enemy has spoken to you], in the name of Jesus. I reject all shame, insecurity, low self-esteem, and feelings of unworthiness, in the name of Jesus. I declare that I am a child of the Most High God, worthy to be loved, cherished, and respected. Father, thank You for healing and restoring my soul and giving me a new beginning. Thank You that according to Proverbs 4:18, my path is shining brighter and brighter until the full day. My brightest days and greatest victories are in my future, not my past. I will become all God created me to be and fulfill every plan and purpose He has for my life. I will enjoy healthy, wonderful, fulfilling relationships. I receive it all by faith with thanksgiving, and it's in the matchless name of Jesus I pray, Amen.

SCRIPTURE REFERENCES

Psalm 103:4
Isaiah 61:3, 7
2 Corinthians 5:17
Psalm 23:3
Psalm 147:3
Jeremiah 18:3–6
Proverbs 4:18

108 Healing from Adultery

HEAVENLY FATHER, I come to You with a broken heart and a crushed spirit from the pain of adultery. Your Word says, "The Lord is close to the brokenhearted; he rescues those whose spirits are crushed," and "He heals the brokenhearted and binds up their wounds." David said, "He restores my soul." Father, I need You to heal my heart and restore my soul. Put Your healing balm on the deep wounds in my soul and heal me supernaturally in a way that only You can.

Thank You that no matter what people do to me, even my own spouse, You will never leave me nor forsake me. I am Your beloved child, and Your love for me is unconditional and unfailing. You will somehow turn what the devil meant for evil to good in my life. You promised to work all things together for my good because I love You and I'm called according to Your purpose. I don't pretend to know how You could turn my husband's/wife's unfaithfulness for good, but I trust that somehow You will.

Lord, just like You forgave the woman caught in the act of adultery, help me to truly forgive [spouse's name]. Your Word commands me to forgive others as You have forgiven me. You never tell us to do anything that You don't give us the ability to do, so I ask for the ability to forgive him/her. Help me to release him/her and the pain he/she caused me. Deliver me from any unforgiveness, bitterness, or toxic thoughts and emotions toward him/her so that my heart can heal and I can move on to the wonderful things You have in my future. I refuse to stay stuck in this pain. Thank You that You redeem my life from destruction. You give me beauty for ashes and the oil of joy for mourning. According to Proverbs 4:18, my brightest days are still in my future.

[If not divorced yet . . .] Father, Your Word says that adultery is a biblical ground for divorce, but it also says that You hate divorce. Divorce is not Your best and would be another trauma in my life. So, I ask for wisdom and guidance from Your Holy Spirit about what to do and how to navigate this situation. Help me to be led by Your Spirit and not my emotions. If it is Your will for me and [spouse's name] to stay together, then I ask You to repair, renew, and remake our marriage better than it was before. Help my husband/wife never to be unfaithful again and earn my trust back. Thank You that You can restore anything and nothing is impossible with You. Bless our marriage and make it a beacon of hope for other marriages and one that brings You glory. I pray all these things in the precious name of Jesus, Amen.

SCRIPTURE REFERENCES

Psalm 34:18 NLT	Ephesians 4:32	Isaiah 61:3
Psalm 147:3 NIV	Matthew 6:14–15	Matthew 5:32
Psalm 23:3	Philippians 3:13–14	Matthew 19:9
Hebrews 13:5	Psalm 103:4	
John 8:3–11	Proverbs 4:18	

109 Healing from Betrayal

HEAVENLY FATHER, I confess to You that my heart is broken, and my spirit crushed from the betrayal of someone/those I trusted. Your Word says, "The Lord is close to the brokenhearted; he rescues those whose spirits are crushed," and "He heals the brokenhearted and binds up their wounds." David said, "He restores my soul." Father, I need You to heal my heart and restore my soul. Put Your healing balm on the deep wounds in my soul, and heal me supernaturally in a way that only You can.

Lord Jesus, thank You that You can empathize with everything I feel because You were betrayed by those closest to You. Your brothers and sisters and those from Your hometown who knew You best did not believe You were the Messiah. Judas, one of Your twelve disciples whom You poured into for three and a half years, betrayed you for money. Peter denied You publicly three times. All Your disciples "forsook [You] and fled." So, You understand the intense pain I feel and have compassion on me.

Help me to see that Judas' betrayal helped You fulfill Your destiny. You would not have been crucified for the sins of the world without his betrayal. Father, thank You that You work all things together for my good. I trust that You will work even painful betrayals for my good somehow.

Father, help me to truly forgive everyone who has betrayed me. Your Word commands me to forgive others as You have forgiven me. So, I choose to forgive them. I release them and the pain they caused me. I pray You would totally deliver me from any unforgiveness, bitterness, or toxic thoughts and emotions toward them. Help me to shake the dust off my feet as You told Your disciples, forget what is past, and, as the apostle Paul wrote, press on toward all the wonderful things You have for my future. Thank You for purging the wrong people out of my life and surrounding me with people who are loyal and trustworthy, people who truly love me and are for me. I pray all these things in the precious name of Jesus, Amen.

SCRIPTURE REFERENCES

Psalm 34:18 NLT	Luke 22:48	Ephesians 4:32
Psalm 147:3 NIV	Matthew 26:69-75	Matthew 6:14-15
Psalm 23:3	Mark 14:50	Matthew 10:14
Jeremiah 8:22	Romans 8:28	Philippians 3:13-14

110 Healing After Divorce

Heavenly Father, I come to You with a broken heart and crushed spirit from my divorce. I have so many emotions swirling around inside—feelings of loss, grief, sadness, failure, fear, and loneliness. I need You like never before. Your Word says, "The Lord is close to the brokenhearted; he rescues those whose spirits are crushed," and "He heals the brokenhearted and binds up their wounds." David wrote, "He restores my soul." Father, I ask You to heal my heart and restore my soul. Put Your healing balm on the deep wounds in my soul and heal me supernaturally in a way that only You can. Thank You that You are my comforter, strengthener, standby, counselor, and healer of my spirit, soul, and body. You have me in the palm of Your hand. You said, "Do not fear, for I am with you; do not be dismayed, for I am your God. I will strengthen you and help you; I will uphold you with my righteous right hand." Thank You that You will never leave nor forsake me. Thank You that I am a victor and never a victim.

Father, You said in Psalm 32:8, "I will instruct you and teach you in the way you should go; I will counsel you with my loving eye on you." I ask You to guide me through this challenging season and bring me into a new season of peace, joy, and victory. Thank You that You redeem my life from destruction and give me beauty for ashes. You said sorrow lasts for a night, but joy comes in the morning; those who sow in tears will reap in joy, and You will turn my mourning into dancing. You're a God of restoration and new beginnings. You said, "Forget the former things; do not dwell on the past. See, I am doing a new thing! Now it springs up; do you not perceive it?" Help me to let go of the pain and disappointments of the past and get ready for the new things You have for me. Thank You that You know the plans You have for me, plans to give me hope and a future.

Father, help me to forgive [name of ex-spouse]. Your Word commands me to forgive others as You have forgiven me, and You never tell us to do something that You don't give us the ability to do. So, I choose to forgive him/her. I release him/her and the pain he/she caused me. I pray that You would completely deliver me from any unforgiveness, bitterness, or other toxic thoughts and emotions toward him/her. I don't want to drag any baggage into the future. I want to be healed and free so that I can lay hold of everything You have for me. Thank You that according to Proverbs 4:18, my path is like the shining sun, shining brighter and brighter until the full day. My brightest days and greatest victories are in my future, not my past! I pray all these things in Jesus' precious name, Amen.

SCRIPTURE REFERENCES

Psalm 34:18 NLT	Psalm 32:8 NIV	Psalm 30:11
Psalm 147:3 NIV	Psalm 103:4	Isaiah 43:18–19 NIV
Psalm 23:3	Isaiah 61:3	Jeremiah 29:11
Isaiah 41:10 NIV	Psalm 30:5	Ephesians 4:32
Deuteronomy 31:8	Psalm 126:5	Proverbs 4:18

111 Healing from Grief

Note: This prayer is not just for grief from loss of a loved one (the next prayer focuses on that), but any kind of grief—divorce, financial reversal, loss of a friendship, etc.

HEAVENLY FATHER, I come to You with a broken heart and crushed spirit from the pain of grief. Thank You that You are my Healer and Deliverer. Your Word says that You heal the brokenhearted and bind up their wounds, and You are close to the brokenhearted and save those who are crushed in spirit. I ask You to heal my broken heart and bind up my wounds. Touch me in the deepest places of my soul and wash away my grief and sorrow by the blood of Jesus. Isaiah 53:4 says, "Surely [Jesus] has borne our griefs and carried our sorrows," so I don't have to carry it anymore. I release all grief, pain, and sorrow to Jesus.

Lord Jesus, You wept at the tomb of Lazarus. You wept over Jerusalem. You had such sorrow in the Garden of Gethsemane that You sweat drops of blood. You were "a man of sorrows, acquainted with deepest grief." Thank You that You can empathize with my grief and have compassion because You experienced grief just like me. Thank You that Your Holy Spirit who lives inside of me is my comforter and strengthener. Though I am walking through a valley right now, You are with me. Your rod and staff comfort me. I will emerge healed, restored, and victorious. Help me to do my part by seeking out a grief support group, counseling, and working with You in prayer to process my grief in a healthy way so that I can be totally healed.

Jesus, You gave me authority over all the power of the enemy. You said whatever I bind on earth will be bound in heaven and whatever I loose on earth will be loosed in heaven. So, I bind, rebuke, cut off, and cast out the spirit of grief, heaviness, sorrow, and every demonic spirit from me, and I loose upon me the joy and peace of the Lord, in Jesus' mighty name.

Father, You promised to give me "beauty for ashes, the oil of joy for mourning, the garment of praise for the spirit of heaviness." You said, "Weeping may endure for a night, but joy comes in the morning," and that You would turn my mourning into dancing. Thank You that You're going to restore my joy and peace, restore my soul, and give me a new beginning. I receive the promise of Proverbs 4:18 that my path is shining brighter and brighter until the full day. My brightest days and greatest victories are in my future, not my past. Thank You that I am healed and free, and I will become all You created me to be and fulfill every plan and purpose You have for me. I pray all these things in the precious name of Jesus, Amen.

SCRIPTURE REFERENCES

Psalm 147:3
Psalm 34:18
Isaiah 53:4
John 11:35
Luke 19:41
Luke 22:44

Isaiah 53:3
Hebrews 4:15
John 14:26
Psalm 23:4
Matthew 18:18
Isaiah 61:3

Psalm 30:5
Psalm 30:11
Psalm 23:3
Proverbs 4:18

112 Healing After Loss of Loved One

HEAVENLY FATHER, thank You for [person's name] and the precious gift he/she was in my life. Thank You for all the lives he/she impacted while he/she was on this earth and for the legacy of [describe their legacy] he/she leaves behind. Most of all, thank You for the promise of eternal life he/she has in Christ Jesus and that he/she is with You in heaven where there is no sickness, pain, or sorrow. Thank You that he/she is more alive and full of joy now than he/she ever was on this earth. Jesus said, "I am the resurrection and the life. He who believes in Me, though he may die, he shall live. And whoever lives and believes in Me shall never die." Thank You that [person's name] just passed from this life to a greater, eternal life. The apostle Paul wrote, "To die is *gain*" and "To depart and be with Christ, which is *better by far*." He also wrote, "Death is swallowed up in victory!" So, thank You that when [person's name] departed this earth, it was the most victorious day of his/her life.

But Father, despite knowing this, my heart is still broken and my spirit is crushed at this loss. Jesus, You were "a man of sorrows, acquainted with deepest grief." You wept at Lazarus' grave. You were so grieved in the Garden of Gethsemane that You sweat drops of blood. So, You understand my loss and grief. Your Word says, "The LORD is close to the brokenhearted; he rescues those whose spirits are crushed," and "He heals the brokenhearted and binds up their wounds." David said, "He restores my soul." Father, I need You to comfort my heart and heal my soul as only You can. Help me to process my grief in a healthy way by seeking out a grief support group or counseling and working with You in prayer so that I can be totally healed.

Your Word says that You are the "God of all comfort, who comforts us in all our tribulation, that we may be able to comfort those who are in any trouble, with the comfort with which we ourselves are comforted by God." I ask for Your comfort, peace, and strength. Let Your shalom peace that surpasses all understanding wash over me and guard my heart and mind through Christ Jesus. Thank You that I have the peace and comfort of knowing that [person's name] is with You in heaven and that I will see him/her again one day. Remind me that I am never alone because You are always with me. You will never leave nor forsake me. Thank You that You will give me beauty for ashes, the oil of joy for mourning, the garment of praise for the spirit of heaviness. You said sorrow lasts for a night, but joy comes in the morning. You said those who sow in tears will reap in joy and promised to turn my mourning into dancing. I receive it by faith with thanksgiving, and it's in Jesus' precious name I pray, Amen.

SCRIPTURE REFERENCES

John 11:25–26
Philippians 1:21, 23 NIV (emphasis added)
1 Corinthians 15:54
Isaiah 53:3 NLT
John 11:35

Luke 22:44
Psalm 34:18 NLT
Psalm 147:3
Psalm 23:3
2 Corinthians 1:3–4

Philippians 4:7
Deuteronomy 31:6
Isaiah 61:3
Psalm 30:5, 11
Psalm 126:5

113 Healing After Miscarriage

HEAVENLY FATHER, I come to You with a broken heart and crushed spirit from the loss of my unborn child. Jesus, You were "a man of sorrows, acquainted with deepest grief." You wept at Lazarus' grave. You were so grieved in the Garden of Gethsemane that You sweat drops of blood. So, You understand my loss and grief. Your Word says, "The Lord is close to the brokenhearted; he rescues those whose spirits are crushed," and "He heals the brokenhearted and binds up their wounds." David said, "He restores my soul." Father, I need You to heal my heart and restore my soul. Put Your healing balm on my soul and heal me supernaturally in a way that only You can.

Your Word says that You are "the Father of mercies and God of all comfort, who comforts us in all our tribulation, that we may be able to comfort those who are in any trouble, with the comfort with which we ourselves are comforted by God." I ask for Your comfort, peace, and strength. Let Your peace that surpasses all understanding wash over me and guard my heart and mind through Christ Jesus. Thank You that I have the peace and comfort of knowing that my baby is with You in heaven and that I will see him/her again one day. Help me to do my part by seeking out a grief support group, counseling, and working with You in prayer to process my grief in a healthy way so that I can be totally healed.

Father, I ask You to heal my body of anything that may have prevented me from having a healthy, full-term pregnancy. Balance all my hormones and heal my womb any way it needs healing. Bless my womb, and I pray that in Your perfect timing I would have a healthy, full-term baby. Thank You that You are a God of redemption and restoration. You will give me beauty for ashes, the oil of joy for mourning. You said sorrow lasts for a night, but joy comes in the morning. You promised to turn my mourning into dancing. I receive it by faith with thanksgiving. In Jesus' precious name I pray, Amen.

SCRIPTURE REFERENCES

Isaiah 53:3 NLT
John 11:35
Luke 22:44

Psalm 34:18 NLT
Psalm 147:3
Psalm 23:3

2 Corinthians 1:3-4
Philippians 4:7
Psalm 30:5, 11

---

114 Healing from Rejection

HEAVENLY FATHER, I confess to You that my heart is broken and my spirit crushed from the pain of rejection. Your Word says, "The Lord is close to the brokenhearted; he rescues those whose spirits are crushed," and "He heals the brokenhearted and binds up their wounds." David said, "He restores my soul." Father, I need You to heal my heart and restore my soul. Put Your healing balm on the deep wounds in my soul and heal me supernaturally in a way that only You can. Thank You that even when people reject me, You promised to neither leave nor forsake me. Psalm 27:10 says that even if my own mother and father reject me, You will never reject me. I am Your beloved child. Your love for me is unconditional and unfailing. You are always for me, never against me.

Lord Jesus, thank You that You can empathize with the pain of rejection because You were rejected by many when You walked the earth, and still are today. Isaiah 53:3 says, "[You were] despised and rejected by men, a man of sorrows and acquainted with grief." John 1:11 says, "He came to His own, and His own did not receive Him." Even Your brothers and sisters and people from Your hometown did not accept You as the Messiah. Your Word says, "He was rejected by people, but he was chosen by God for great honor." So, You know what it's like to be rejected. You understand the pain I feel and have compassion on me.

Father, help me to truly forgive everyone who has rejected me. Your Word commands me to forgive others as You have forgiven me. So, I choose to forgive them. I release them and the pain they caused me. I pray You would deliver me completely from any unforgiveness, bitterness, or any toxic thoughts and emotions toward them. Help me to shake the dust off, as You told Your disciples, forget what is past, like the apostle Paul wrote, and press on toward all the wonderful things You have for my future. Thank You for purging the wrong people out of my life and surrounding me with people who are loyal and trustworthy, people who truly love me, believe in me, and are for me. I pray all these things in the precious name of Jesus, Amen.

SCRIPTURE REFERENCES

Psalm 34:18 NLT	Psalm 27:10	Ephesians 4:32
Psalm 147:3 NIV	Isaiah 53:3	Matthew 6:14–15
Psalm 23:3	John 1:11	Matthew 10:14
Hebrews 13:5	1 Peter 2:4 NLT	Philippians 3:13–14

115 Healing from Sexual Assault

HEAVENLY FATHER, I come to You with a broken heart and a crushed spirit from the pain of sexual assault. Jesus, You were "a man of sorrows, acquainted with deepest grief." Your body was assaulted in a different way, as You were beaten with thirty-seven lashes and hung on a cross to die. I know You understand the deep pain in my soul from the violation of my body. Your Word says, "The Lord is close to the brokenhearted; he rescues those whose spirits are crushed," and "He heals the brokenhearted and binds up their wounds." David said, "He restores my soul." Father, I need You to heal my heart and restore my shattered soul. Put Your healing balm on the deep wounds in my soul and heal me supernaturally in a way that only You can. I ask You to heal me so completely that I can remove the protective walls around my heart, have healthy relationships, and love like if I've never been hurt.

Thank You that You can take what the devil meant for evil and turn it into good in our lives. You promised to work all things together for good for those who love You and are called according to Your purpose. I ask You to turn what was done to me for good somehow. Make the enemy pay for what he did to me and turn my trauma into a testimony that will bring You glory and help others.

Father, help me to truly forgive the person/people who sexually abused me [name his/her/their name(s) if you know]. Your Word commands me to forgive others as You have forgiven me. You never tell us to do anything that You don't give us the ability to do, so I ask for the ability to forgive him/her/them. Help me to release him/her/them and the pain he/she/they caused me. Deliver me from any unforgiveness, bitterness, or any toxic thoughts and emotions toward him/her/them so that my heart can heal, and I can move on to the wonderful things You have in my future. I refuse to stay stuck in this pain. Thank You that You redeem my life from destruction. You give me beauty for ashes and the oil of joy for mourning. Thank You for healing my soul and that, according to Proverbs 4:18, my brightest days are still in my future. I pray all these things in Jesus' precious name, Amen.

SCRIPTURE REFERENCES

Isaiah 53:3 NLT	Psalm 23:3	Psalm 103:4
Psalm 34:18 NLT	Romans 8:28	Isaiah 61:3
Psalm 147:3 NIV	Ephesians 4:32	Proverbs 4:18

116 Healing from Trauma

HEAVENLY FATHER, thank You that You are my Healer and Deliverer. You heal the brokenhearted and bind up their wounds. I ask You to heal me of every trauma, soul wound, and painful memory. Touch me in the deepest places of my soul—the hurt pockets that no one knows about, the scars inflicted by other people and life, the memories that are too painful to share, even the traumas and pains I don't consciously remember—and wash them away by the blood of Jesus. Thank You that Jesus took my pain and sorrow upon Himself at the cross and I don't have to carry it anymore. I release all trauma, pain, and sorrow to You. By Jesus' wounds I was healed—spirit, soul, and body.

Father, Your Word commands me to forgive others just as You have forgiven me in Christ Jesus. Help me to forgive and release anyone who traumatized me, understanding that forgiveness is critical for my own healing. Help me to release all bitterness and toxic emotions and receive the total freedom that comes from letting go. The apostle Paul wrote, "I focus on this one thing: Forgetting the past . . . I press on." Help me let go of the past so that I can lay hold of the wonderful things You have for my future.

Father, thank You for Your many promises of restoration. You said in Psalm 23:3 that You restore my soul. I ask You to replace all the pain in my soul with Your love, peace, and joy. You promised to give me beauty for ashes, the oil of joy for mourning, the garment of praise for heaviness. Help me to give You the ashes in my life so I can receive Your beauty, mourning so I can receive Your joy, and heaviness so I can have a fresh praise. Thank You that I am not defined by what happened to me, and I don't have to be stuck. You have a new beginning for me. You promised to turn what the devil meant for evil to good in my life and give me a twofold recompense for my former shame. You promised to restore the years the swarming locusts have eaten. I ask You to give me back all the years that were stolen through trauma.

Father, thank You that Proverbs 4:18 says my path is shining brighter and brighter until the full day. My brightest days and greatest victories are in my future, not my past. Thank You that I am healed and free, and I will become all You created me to be and fulfill every plan and purpose You have for me. I pray all these things in the precious name of Jesus, Amen.

SCRIPTURE REFERENCES

Psalm 147:3	Philippians 3:13–14 NLT	Joel 2:25
Isaiah 53:4–5	Psalm 23:3	Proverbs 4:18
Ephesians 4:32	Isaiah 61:3, 7	

VIII
FREEDOM

117 General Prayer for Freedom

HEAVENLY FATHER, I come to You asking for freedom from every stronghold, bondage, addiction, bad habit, generational curse, lie, wrong belief, limiting mindset, [name anything specific you need freedom from], and everything that holds me back from being all You created me to be. I repent for every sin, lie, and wrong belief that gave the enemy legal access to attack and oppress me. I ask You to forgive me, cleanse me of all unrighteousness, and close every door to the enemy. Thank You that Jesus came to set captives free and proclaim liberty to those who are bound. "For freedom, Christ set [me] free." "If the Son sets [me] free, [I] will be free indeed." By faith, I receive the freedom Jesus died to give me. I ask You to break every chain off me, in the mighty name of Jesus.

Father, Your Word says that we are transformed by the renewing of our mind. Help me to renew my mind with what You say about me—that Jesus has set me free, that in all things I am more than a conqueror, and that I can do all things through Christ who strengthens me. Help me to embrace my new identity as free and victorious in Christ.

Father, I repent for the sins of my ancestors that opened the door to any generational curses, addictions, or defeated mindsets. I ask You to forgive every sin of my ancestors and cleanse my family line by the blood of Jesus. You said, "If anyone is in Christ, he is a new creation; old things have passed away; behold, all things have become new." Thank You that I have a new bloodline and lineage in Christ Jesus and that every generational curse has passed away. Jesus has redeemed me from every curse. I break, cut off, renounce, revoke, and nullify every generational curse, in Jesus' mighty name! The weapons of my warfare are not carnal but mighty in God for the pulling down of strongholds. So, in the name of Jesus, I pull down, demolish, and shatter every stronghold in my life. I bind, rebuke, and cast out every demonic spirit from me, in Jesus' name! I revoke, renounce, and sever every agreement and association with the forces of darkness, in Jesus' name.

Lord, help me to stand firm in the liberty for which You set me free and not be entangled again with a yoke of bondage. Empower me to become everything You created me to be and to fulfill every plan and purpose You have for my life. I pray all of this in the precious name of Jesus, Amen.

SCRIPTURE REFERENCES

1 John 1:9	Romans 12:2	Galatians 3:13
Luke 4:18	Romans 8:37	2 Corinthians 10:4
Galatians 5:1 CSB	Philippians 4:13	
John 8:36 ESV	2 Corinthians 5:17	

118 Freedom from Addiction

Heavenly Father, I come to You asking for freedom from addiction to [name the addiction(s)]. I repent for engaging in this/these addiction(s). I ask You to forgive me, cleanse me of all unrighteousness, and close every door to the enemy. Thank You that I don't have to overcome this/these addiction(s) in my own strength or willpower. Jesus came to set captives free and proclaim liberty to all those who are bound. "For freedom, Christ set [me] free." "If the Son sets [me] free, [I] will be free indeed." By faith, I receive the freedom that Jesus died to give me. I ask You to break every chain of addiction off me, in the mighty name of Jesus. I pray You would so radically deliver me that not only would I never desire [name addiction(s)] again, but I would have an aversion to it/them. You said, "Ask and you shall receive," and I ask that I would be repelled and disgusted by the very thing(s) to which I had an addiction.

Father, Your Word says that we are transformed by the renewing of our mind. Help me to renew my mind with what Your Word says about me—that Jesus has set me free, that in all things I am more than a conqueror, and that I can do all things through Christ who strengthens me. Help me to reject my old identity as someone with an addiction and embrace my new identity as free and victorious in Christ. I ask You to heal and deliver my brain from the dopamine cycle that causes me to crave [name addiction(s)]. Your Word says that You heal, deliver, and make all things new. So, I ask You to heal my dopamine receptors and reset my brain to how it was before this addiction started. Give me a healthy, normal brain and break the cycle of addiction in my life forever, in Jesus' name.

Father, I repent for the sins of my ancestors that opened the door to a generational stronghold of addiction. I ask You to forgive every sin of my ancestors and cleanse my family line by the blood of Jesus. You said, "If anyone is in Christ, he is a new creation; old things have passed away; behold, all things have become new." Thank You that I have a new bloodline and lineage in Christ Jesus and every generational curse has passed away. Jesus has redeemed me from every curse. I break, cut off, renounce, revoke, and nullify every generational curse of addiction to [name addiction(s)], in Jesus' mighty name! The weapons of my warfare are not carnal but mighty in God for the pulling down of strongholds. So, in the name of Jesus, I pull down, demolish, and shatter the stronghold of addiction. I bind, rebuke, and cast out every spirit of addiction and bondage from me, in Jesus' name! I revoke, renounce, and sever every agreement and association with the forces of darkness, in Jesus' name.

Lord, with Your help I will stand firm in the liberty for which You set me free and not be entangled again with a yoke of bondage. I am free in You and will become everything You created me to be. I pray all of this in the precious name of Jesus, Amen.

> **SCRIPTURE REFERENCES**
> 1 John 1:9
> Luke 4:18
> Galatians 5:1 CSB
> John 8:36 ESV
> Romans 12:2
> Romans 8:37
> Philippians 4:13
> 2 Corinthians 5:17
> Galatians 3:3
> 2 Corinthians 10:4
> Galatians 5:1

119 Freedom from Anger

HEAVENLY FATHER, I come to You seeking freedom from anger. Your Word says, "Everyone should be quick to listen, slow to speak and slow to become angry, because human anger does not produce the righteousness that God desires." It says, "Don't let your spirit rush to be angry, for anger abides in the heart of fools." Lord, I don't want to be bound by anger or be a quick-tempered fool. I repent for having ungodly anger, hostility, and aggression in my life. I repent for trying to control people and situations through anger. I repent for the times I have been angry at You. I ask You to forgive me, wash me clean by the blood of Jesus, and close every door to the enemy. Thank You that Jesus came to set me free from all captivity and oppression. Whom the Son sets free is free indeed! I don't want to be held captive or oppressed by anger anymore. So, I ask You to break every chain of anger off me, in Jesus' name. Instead of anger, fill me with the Holy Spirit and His fruit of love, joy, peace, patience, kindness, gentleness, faithfulness, and self-control.

Father, I repent for the sins of my ancestors that may have opened the door to a generational stronghold of anger. I ask You to forgive every sin of my ancestors and cleanse my family line by the blood of Jesus. You said, "If anyone is in Christ, he is a new creation; old things have passed away; behold, all things have become new." Thank You that I have a new bloodline and lineage in Christ Jesus and every generational curse has passed away. Jesus has redeemed me from every curse. I break, cut off, renounce, revoke, and nullify every generational curse of anger, in Jesus' mighty name! The weapons of my warfare are not carnal but mighty in God for the pulling down of strongholds. So, in the name of Jesus, I pull down, demolish, and shatter the stronghold of anger. I command every spirit of anger, hostility, and aggression to leave me now and never come back, in Jesus' name!

Father, thank You for the freedom and victory I have in Christ Jesus. Thank You that I will not be bound and controlled by anger any longer, but I will walk in Your unshakable shalom peace. Thank You that You are in the business of transforming lives and the people closest to me will notice the transformation in me. I pray all these things in the mighty name of Jesus, Amen.

SCRIPTURE REFERENCES

James 1:19–20 NIV	John 8:36	Galatians 3:13
Ecclesiastes 7:9 CSB	Galatians 5:22	2 Corinthians 10:4
Luke 4:18	2 Corinthians 5:17	

120 Freedom from Anxiety

Heavenly Father, I come to You asking to be set free from anxiety. Jesus came to set the captives and oppressed free. I don't want to be held captive and oppressed by anxiety anymore. I ask that today would be the day I break free and start living with a peaceful, calm mind and confident trust in You. Father, Your Word commands us to "be anxious for nothing, but in everything by prayer and supplication, with thanksgiving, let your requests be made known to God; and the peace of God, which surpasses all understanding, will guard your hearts and minds through Christ Jesus." It also tells us to "[cast] the whole of your care [all your anxieties, all your worries, all your concerns, once and for all] on Him, for He cares for you affectionately and . . . watchfully." Help me to be a doer of Your Word and truly cast my anxieties and cares upon You and refuse to be anxious. Thank You that when I do that, Your shalom peace will guard my heart and mind from all anxiety. Thank You that You care for me affectionately and watchfully. You are on the throne, in control, and have me in the palm of Your hand. There is no reason for me to be anxious or afraid.

Your Word says, "You will keep him in perfect peace whose mind is stayed on You because he trusts in You." Help me to keep my mind stayed on You rather than on my problems and things that cause anxiety, so I can enjoy Your perfect peace. Help me to trust You with my whole heart. Instead of anxiety, empower me to walk in faith, have a victorious mindset, declare Your promises, and exercise my authority in Christ over the enemy. Thank You that when I lie down to sleep at night, my mind and emotions won't be tormented by anxiety, but I will sleep like a baby, knowing that You are fighting my battles and perfecting everything that concerns me.

Father, I repent for entertaining a spirit of anxiety when You command me to be anxious for nothing. I ask You to forgive me, cleanse me by the blood of Jesus, and close every door to the enemy. I bind, cut off, and cast out every spirit of anxiety, fear, worry, dread, panic attacks, and foreboding from me, in the mighty name of Jesus. I command those spirits to leave me and never come back, in Jesus' name. I break, sever, renounce, and revoke all agreements and associations with the spirits of anxiety, fear, worry, dread, panic attacks, and foreboding, in Jesus' name. I loose upon me unshakable shalom peace, a calm mind and spirit, and confident trust in God, in the name of Jesus. Father, thank You that I am free from anxiety, and I will walk in divine peace, faith, and victory from now on. In Jesus' precious name I pray, Amen.

SCRIPTURE REFERENCES

Luke 4:18	Isaiah 26:3	Psalm 138:8
Philippians 4:6–7	Proverbs 3:5	
1 Peter 5:7 AMPC	Exodus 14:14	

121 Freedom from Bitterness

HEAVENLY FATHER, Your Word says, "Make sure that no one falls short of the grace of God and that no root of bitterness springs up, causing trouble and defiling many." Father, I repent for allowing bitterness to fester in my soul and defile me. Peter told a man in Acts 8:23, "I see that you are poisoned by bitterness." I repent for allowing bitterness to poison my thoughts, attitudes, and interactions with people. I repent for unresolved offense, resentment, anger, unforgiveness, and disappointment in my soul that developed into bitterness. I ask You to forgive me, wash me clean by the blood of Jesus, heal and restore my soul, and close every door to the enemy. Thank You that Jesus came to set me free from all captivity and oppression. Whom the Son sets free is free indeed! I don't want to be held captive or oppressed by bitterness anymore. I ask You to break every chain of bitterness off me, in Jesus' name. Pull up bitterness by the root and remove it far from me.

Father, thank You that the weapons of my warfare are not carnal but mighty in You for the pulling down of strongholds. So, in the name of Jesus, I pull down, demolish, and shatter the stronghold of bitterness. I command every spirit of bitterness, unforgiveness, offense, resentment, anger, and disappointment to leave me now and never come back, in Jesus' name! Lord, instead of bitterness, fill me afresh and anew with Your Holy Spirit, and help me to walk in His fruit of love, joy, peace, kindness, and goodness.

Father, Your Word commands me to forgive others just as You have forgiven me in Christ Jesus. I choose right now to forgive everyone who has ever hurt me and release them and the pain they caused me. I let go of the hurt, offense, anger, resentment, and bitterness. I let go of disappointment from what didn't work out or go my way. Thank You that You redeem my life from destruction, give me beauty for ashes, and turn what the devil meant for evil in my life to good. So, I let go of everything from the past that caused me to be bitter, and I receive Your freedom, peace, joy, and victory. By faith, I look ahead to the wonderful things You have in store for my future. I will live my best life and become all You created me to be. I pray all these things in Jesus' mighty name, Amen.

SCRIPTURE REFERENCES

Hebrews 12:15 CSB
Acts 8:23
John 8:36
2 Corinthians 10:4
Ephesians 4:32
Psalm 103:4
Isaiah 61:3
Genesis 50:20

122 Freedom from Comparison

HEAVENLY FATHER, Your Word says that when we compare ourselves to others, we are unwise. I ask You to set me free from comparing myself or my life to others. Remind me that You made me a unique, original masterpiece unlike anyone else. You created me with a divine purpose that is unlike anybody else's and gave me everything I need to fulfill it. You chose my gender, ethnicity, looks, personality, talents, abilities, when and where I would be born, which family I would be born into, and everything about me. You made me exactly the way You wanted me. I am complete in You, lacking nothing, so there is no need for me to look at others and be insecure or covet anything about them. Help me to love and embrace who You uniquely created me to be and resist the temptation of comparison.

Your Word says, "Make a careful exploration of who you are and the work you have been given, and then sink yourself into that. . . . Don't compare yourself with others. Each of you must take responsibility for doing the creative best you can with your own life." Help me to become the best version of myself instead of wishing I was like someone else. Free me from looking at other people's lives—their money, possessions, vacations, career, marriage, children, appearance, or anything else—and comparing them to mine. Help me to live with a spirit of gratitude for all You have given me and be genuinely happy when You bless others. You are not short on blessings; there is enough for everybody. Nobody can take the blessings You have for me.

Deliver me once and for all from comparison, competition and covetousness. Your Word says, "Set your gaze on the path before you. With fixed purpose, looking straight ahead, ignore life's distractions." Help me to see that falling for the comparison trap is not only a distraction but folly. I am the most anointed person on the planet to be me, but I am not anointed to be someone else or run someone else's race. Empower me to run my own race and become the best version of myself. I pray all these things in Jesus' precious name, Amen.

SCRIPTURE REFERENCES
2 Corinthians 10:12
Galatians 6:4-5 MSG
Ephesians 3:20
Proverbs 4:25 TPT

123 Freedom from Criticalness

HEAVENLY FATHER, I come to You asking to be set free from criticalness. Thank You that Jesus came to set me free from all captivity and oppression. Whom the Son sets free is free indeed! I don't want to be held captive or oppressed by criticalness anymore. I want to be free from everything that is a stumbling block in my life. So, I ask You to break every chain of criticalness off me, in Jesus' name. Your Word says, "Be imitators of God as dear children." You are not a critical, judgmental God but a positive, loving, gracious God. Help me to imitate You as Your child and representative on earth. Help me to think Your thoughts about myself, other people, and the world, and be loving and accepting, not critical.

Father, I repent for the sins of my ancestors that may have opened the door to a generational stronghold of criticalness. I ask You to forgive every sin, iniquity, and transgression of my ancestors and cleanse my family line by the blood of Jesus. You said, "If anyone is in Christ, he is a new creation; old things have passed away; behold, all things have become new." Thank You that I have a new bloodline and lineage in Christ Jesus, and every generational curse has passed away. Jesus has redeemed me from every curse. I break, cut off, renounce, revoke, and nullify every generational curse of criticalness, in Jesus' mighty name! The weapons of my warfare are not carnal but mighty in God for the pulling down of strongholds, casting down arguments and every high thing that exalts itself against the knowledge of God. So, in the name of Jesus, I pull down, demolish, and shatter the stronghold of criticalness. I command the spirit of criticalness to leave me now and never come back, in Jesus' name! I cast down every critical, judgmental thought in my mind and cover my mind and thoughts with the blood of Jesus.

Father, help me to be transformed by the renewing of my mind. Train me to focus on the good in life, the world, and people rather than the bad. Help me to have a victorious mindset and only think on things that are positive, faith-filled, victorious, and worthy of praise. Thank You that I am free from criticalness forever, and I will be known as a loving, accepting, and Christlike person. I pray all these things in the precious name of Jesus, Amen.

SCRIPTURE REFERENCES

Luke 4:18 CSB
John 8:36
Ephesians 5:1

Ephesians 4:29
2 Corinthians 5:17
Galatians 3:13

2 Corinthians 10:4–6
Romans 12:2
Philippians 4:8

124 Freedom from Depression

HEAVENLY FATHER, I come to You asking for freedom from depression. I repent for believing any lies, entertaining wrong thoughts and emotions, and engaging in any sins that opened the door to depression in my life. I ask You to forgive me, wash me clean by the blood of Jesus, and close every door to the enemy.

Your Word says, "Submit to God. Resist the devil and he will flee from you." I submit my mind, emotions, and entire being to You, and I resist the devil, and he must flee from me. You said that You have not given me a spirit of fear, but of power, love, and a *sound mind*. So, give me a healthy, sound, peaceful mind. Help me to have the mind of Christ, take every thought captive, and reject every thought that doesn't line up with Your Word. Let Your shalom peace that surpasses all understanding guard my heart and mind through Christ Jesus. Let it wash over me and invade every part of my being

Father, thank You that Jesus came to set the captives free and proclaim liberty to those who are bound and oppressed. Whom the Son sets free is free indeed! So, I ask You to break every chain of depression, mental torment, and suicidal thoughts off me, in Jesus' mighty name. Thank You that You have given me authority over all the power of the enemy. The devil and his demons are subject to me in Your name. Whatever I bind on earth will be bound in heaven. So, I bind, rebuke, cut off, and cast out every spirit of depression, heaviness, sadness, hopelessness, oppression, suicide, lying, and every demonic spirit from me, in the mighty name of Jesus. Father, You said, "The Lord is faithful, who will establish you and guard you from the evil one." I ask You to guard me from the evil one. Put Your mighty hedge of protection around me and my mind that the enemy cannot penetrate. I cover my mind and every part of my being with the blood of Jesus. No weapon formed against me shall prosper.

Father, I repent for the sins of my ancestors that may have opened the door to a generational stronghold of depression. I ask You to forgive every sin, iniquity, and transgression of my ancestors and cleanse my family line by the blood of Jesus. You said, "If anyone is in Christ, he is a new creation; old things have passed away; behold, all things have become new." Thank You that I have a new bloodline and lineage in Christ Jesus, and every generational curse has passed away. Jesus has redeemed me from every curse.

I break, cut off, renounce, revoke, and nullify every generational curse of depression, in Jesus' mighty name! The weapons of my warfare are not carnal but mighty in God for the pulling down of strongholds, casting down arguments and every high thing that exalts itself against the knowledge of God. So, in the name of Jesus, I pull down, demolish, and shatter the stronghold of depression!

Father, if there is something in my physiology that needs healing, I ask You to heal me. Balance my hormones and neurotransmitters and cause them to be at optimal levels. Heal and balance my gut microbiome. Give me divine instruction about anything I need to do to heal my body. Help me to do my part to defeat depression and foster good mental health by eating a healthy diet, exercising regularly, getting outside in sunlight and nature every day, and having meaningful community with others. Thank You that I am free from depression. I am healthy, peaceful, free, and victorious in Christ Jesus. I pray all these things in Jesus' precious name, Amen.

SCRIPTURE REFERENCES

James 4:7	John 8:36	2 Thessalonians 3:3
2 Timothy 1:7	Galatians 5:1	Luke 10:17, 19
1 Corinthians 2:16	Isaiah 54:17	Matthew 18:18
Philippians 4:7	2 Corinthians 5:17	Job 1:10
Luke 4:18	2 Corinthians 10:4–5	

125 Freedom from Disappointment

HEAVENLY FATHER, I come to You confessing that I feel deeply disappointed about circumstances in my life, certain people, and even You at times. I repent for giving into disappointment, agreeing with the lies of the enemy, and taking on a victim spirit and self-pity. I repent for any disappointment and anger I have had toward You. You are perfect and holy in all Your ways and not to blame for my disappointments. I ask You to forgive me, wash me clean by the blood of Jesus, and deliver me from the grip of disappointment. David wrote, "Why am I discouraged? Why is my heart so sad? I will put my hope in God! I will praise him again—my Savior and my God!" Help me to hope in You, stay in faith, and keep a positive attitude, knowing that You promised to work all things together for my good, even disappointments and setbacks.

Father, Your Word instructs us to let our minds dwell only on what is true, right, pure, lovely, excellent, and worthy of praise. Help my mind to focus on what is right and worthy of praise in my life. Help me to be thankful for what I have and what is good in my life instead of focusing on what I don't have and what is not good. Remind me that everybody faces disappointments in life and that billions of people in the world are worse off than me and would gladly trade places with me. You didn't promise us a trouble-free life where we always get our way. Jesus said, "Here on earth you *will* have many trials and sorrows. But take heart, because I have overcome the world." Help me to take heart and remember that You are on the throne, You have me in the palm of Your hand, and if I stay in faith and keep a good attitude, You will turn it all around.

Father, Your Word says that You restore our soul. I ask You to put Your healing balm on my heart and restore my soul from disappointment. Restore my peace, joy, and hope. Renew a steadfast spirit within me. The apostle Paul said, "One thing I do, forgetting those things which are behind and reaching forward to those things which are ahead." Help me to let go of what didn't work out and press on to the wonderful things You have in my future. Help me to be resilient, shake off disappointment, and have faith and expectancy for a divine turnaround. I pray all these things in Jesus' precious name, Amen.

SCRIPTURE REFERENCES

Psalm 42:11 NLT
Romans 8:28
Philippians 4:8

John 16:33 NLT
(emphasis added)
Psalm 23:3

Psalm 51:10, 12
Philippians 3:13

126 Freedom from Eating Disorders

HEAVENLY FATHER, I come to You asking for freedom from eating disorders [name eating disorder]. I repent for believing lies, having wrong beliefs and mindsets, and engaging in behaviors with food that are destructive to my body and mental health. I ask You to forgive me, cleanse me of all unrighteousness, and close every door to the enemy. Thank You that I don't have to overcome [name eating disorder] in my own strength or willpower. Jesus came "to proclaim freedom to the captives and . . . set free the oppressed." "For freedom, Christ set [me] free." "If the Son sets [me] free, [I] will be free indeed." By faith, I receive the freedom that Jesus died to give me. I ask You to break every chain of [name eating disorder] off me and radically set me free, in the mighty name of Jesus.

Father, Your Word says that we are transformed by the renewing of our mind. Heal my mind and perception of myself so that I don't see myself in a distorted way. Invade my mind with Your light and truth. Help me to see myself as You see me—beautiful, fearfully, and wonderfully made, a masterpiece created by Your own hands. Help me to love myself and my body just the way I am, as You do. Help me not to abuse food in any way but to have a healthy relationship with it. I repent for using food as a means of control because it is one thing that I have total control over. I realize that the enemy lured me in with this lie and used it to control me. Father, I yield control of everything in my life to You.

Your Word says to submit to You; to resist the devil, and he must flee from me. So, I submit my body, mind, will, and everything in my life to You. I resist the devil, and according to Your Word, he must flee from me.

Thank You that You gave me authority over all the power of the enemy and whatever I bind on earth will be bound in heaven. So, I bind, rebuke, cut off, and cast out every spirit of [name eating disorder], lies, control, torment, bondage, oppression, and every demonic spirit, in Jesus' mighty name. Go from me and never come back, in Jesus' name. I renounce, revoke, and sever every agreement and association with the spirit of [name eating disorder] and all the forces of darkness, in Jesus' name. The weapons of my warfare are not carnal but mighty in God for the pulling down of strongholds. So, in the name of Jesus, I pull down, demolish, and shatter the stronghold of [name eating disorder] and every demonic stronghold in my life.

Thank You that I am free and victorious in Christ over [name eating disorder]. Thank You that my mind is healthy, my relationship with food is healthy, and my self-image is healthy. I will become all You created me to be and fulfill every plan You have for my life. I pray all these things in Jesus' mighty name, Amen.

SCRIPTURE REFERENCES

1 John 1:9	John 8:36 ESV	Luke 10:19
Luke 4:18 HCSB	Romans 12:2	Matthew 18:18
Galatians 5:1 CSB	James 4:7	2 Corinthians 10:4

127 Freedom from Fear

HEAVENLY FATHER, You commanded us 365 times in Your Word not to fear. I repent for entertaining fearful thoughts and emotions. I ask You to forgive me and set me free from all fear. You said that You have not given us a spirit of fear, but of power, love, and a sound mind. So, I revoke, renounce, and sever every agreement with the spirit of fear, in the name of Jesus. According to the authority given to me in Luke 10:19, I command the spirit of fear to leave me and never come back, in Jesus' name. I pull down the stronghold of fear and cast down every fearful thought and imagination, in the name of Jesus.

Thank You, Father, that You have me in the palm of Your hand. You protect me and fight my battles. You surround me with mighty angels. I have nothing to fear. So, I reject fear in all its forms and refuse to be in bondage to fear. Jesus Christ has set me free!

Your Word says, "Perfect love casts out fear." Thank You that Your perfect love casts out all fear from me. Help me to fully receive Your love. Let it wash over me and extinguish all fear that seeks to impose itself in my life. Even when I walk through the darkest valley, I will not fear because You are with me. You will never leave nor forsake me. Your rod and staff comfort me. Instead of fear, anxiety, and worry, I receive Your divine peace that surpasses all understanding to guard my heart and mind through Christ Jesus. I pray all these things in the name of Jesus Christ, the Prince of Peace, Amen.

SCRIPTURE REFERENCES

Isaiah 41:10, 13	Luke 10:19	1 John 4:18
Deuteronomy 31:6, 8	Romans 8:15	Psalm 23
2 Timothy 1:7	Isaiah 49:16	Philippians 4:7

128 Freedom from Guilt, Shame, Condemnation

HEAVENLY FATHER, Your Word says, "All have sinned and fall short of the glory of God, being justified freely by [Your] grace through the redemption that is in Christ Jesus." Thank You that You loved me while I was yet a sinner and sent Jesus to die on the cross for my sins. I am justified freely by Your grace. I couldn't earn it, and I didn't deserve it; it was a free gift because You love me. Your Word says, "[You] made [Jesus] who knew no sin to be sin for us, that we might become the righteousness of God in Him." Thank You for the great exchange where Jesus took my sins and gave me His righteousness. I became the perfect righteousness of God in Him. When You look at me, You don't see my sins, mistakes, and failures. You see me as perfectly blameless because of the blood of Jesus.

Colossians 2:14 says, "[Jesus] canceled the record of the charges against [me] and took it away by nailing it to the cross." Every charge or accusation the devil had on me or ever will was nailed to the cross and canceled by Jesus. Though my sins are like scarlet, You made them white as snow. You removed my sins from me as far as the east is from the west and remember them no more. I am totally free from all guilt, condemnation, shame, and feelings of unworthiness because of Jesus' finished work on the cross. Your Word says, "There is no condemnation for those who are in Christ Jesus" and that I am accepted and approved in the Beloved.

Father, set me free from any feelings of guilt, condemnation, shame, or unworthiness. Help me to reject all accusations, lies, and wrong beliefs, and help me to walk in my identity as a blood-bought, blood-washed child of the Most High God. Help me to live with a confident mindset that I am totally righteous and blameless before You. Thank You for loving me so extravagantly that

You sent Jesus to die for me and remove my guilt, shame, and condemnation forever. I pray all these things in the precious name of Jesus, Amen.

SCRIPTURE REFERENCES

Romans 3:23–24
2 Corinthians 5:21
Colossians 2:14 NLT
Isaiah 1:18
Psalm 103:12
Hebrews 8:12
Romans 8:1
Ephesians 1:6

129 Freedom from Insecurity

HEAVENLY FATHER, Your Word says, "It is for freedom that Christ has set us free," and "If the Son sets you free, you are truly free." Thank You that Jesus has set me free from insecurity or anything else that would try to hold me back from being all You created me to be. Help me to reject all insecurity and feelings of unworthiness or inadequacy and walk in the freedom Jesus died to give me. Help me to put my shoulders back, hold my head up high, and walk confidently in my identity in Christ. Give me a godly self-image and self-esteem that aligns with Your Word.

Father, I think about how Moses was insecure because he stuttered, but You said, "Who has made man's mouth? . . . I will be with your mouth and teach you what you shall say." Gideon said, "My clan is the weakest in Manasseh, and I am the least in my father's house," but You called him a mighty man of valor. When You called Jeremiah to be a prophet, he said, "I cannot speak, for I am a youth," but You said, "Before I formed you in the womb I knew you; . . . I ordained you a prophet to the nations. . . . Do not say, 'I am a youth.'" These men demonstrated what Your Word says, that "our sufficiency is from God." You created me, You are with me, and You will help me accomplish whatever You call me to do. So, there is no place for insecurity in my life!

Father, I repent for entertaining lies from the enemy and thoughts that opened the door to insecurity. Your Word tells us to be transformed by the renewing of our mind. Help me to renew my mind daily with Your Word, believe only what it says about me, and reject any thoughts to the contrary. Your Word says that I am fearfully and wonderfully made by You, the Creator of the universe. You knit me together in my mother's womb and made me exactly the way You wanted me. You are perfect in all Your ways; You don't make mistakes or create anyone inferior. I am a unique masterpiece created in Your image and likeness. You put Your DNA inside of me. I have royal blood flowing through my veins. I bind, break, cancel, and nullify every generational curse, stronghold, lie, and wrong belief associated with insecurity, in the name of Jesus. Thank You that I am free from all insecurity and will live confidently and securely in Christ. I pray all these things in Jesus' name, Amen.

SCRIPTURE REFERENCES

Galatians 5:1 NIV	Exodus 4:11–12	2 Corinthians 3:5
John 8:36 NLT	Judges 6:15, 12	Romans 12:2
Psalm 139:14	Jeremiah 1:5–7	Psalm 139:13, 14

130 Freedom from Lack, Poverty

HEAVENLY FATHER, thank You that You are not a God of lack and poverty but a God of abundance and prosperity. When You created Adam and Eve, You placed them in a lush Garden full of abundance where they lacked for nothing. When You led the

Israelites to the Promised Land in Canaan, You described it as "a land in which you will eat bread without scarcity, in which you will lack nothing." Deuteronomy 8:18 says that You give us the power to get wealth. Abraham, Isaac, Jacob, Joseph, Job, David, Solomon, Esther, and Ruth were all wealthy. Your gates in heaven are made of pearl, and Your streets are paved with gold. The earth is Yours and the fullness thereof. You have an unlimited supply, and there is no lack with You. You said there is no lack for those who seek You. Psalm 34:10 says, "The young lions lack and suffer hunger; but those who seek the Lord shall not lack any good thing." Psalm 23:1 says, "The Lord is my shepherd; I shall not [lack]." So, Father, I ask You to deliver me from all lack and poverty. Help me to have abundance so that I can build Your Kingdom and be a conduit of Your blessings to others.

Father, deliver me from any lack or poverty mindset. Help me to have a big, Kingdom mindset. Set me free from any spirit of religion that has made me believe lies that You don't want me to prosper financially or that You don't care about such things. Help me to dig into Your Word and renew my mind with what You say about prosperity and abundance, not what man says. Father, I repent for the sins of my ancestors and my own sins that may have opened the door to poverty and lack. I ask You to forgive every sin of poor money management, greed, love of money, gambling, money gained through illegal or illicit means, or any other sin involving money. Cleanse my family line and me of all those sins, iniquities, and transgressions by the blood of Jesus. You said, "If anyone is in Christ, this person is a new creation; the old things passed away; behold, new things have come." Thank You that I have a new bloodline and lineage in Christ Jesus. Every old generational curse and stronghold involving money has passed away. Jesus has redeemed me from every curse. So, in the name of Jesus, I break, cut off, renounce, revoke, and nullify every generational curse of poverty, lack, poor money management, or any other curse involving money.

Father, I say "yes and amen" to all Your promises of prosperity and abundance. You said, "Wherever you go and whatever you do, you will be blessed. . . . The LORD will guarantee a blessing on everything you do and will fill your storehouses with grain. The LORD . . . will bless all the work you do. You will lend . . . but you will never need to borrow. . . . The LORD will make you the head and not the tail, and you will always be on top and never at the bottom." Your Word says, "God is able to make all grace abound toward you, that you, always having all sufficiency in all things, may have an abundance for every good work." I ask for Your grace to abound toward me so that I can have that abundance for every good work, build Your Kingdom, and bring You glory. Thank You that I am a no-lack person and that I will enjoy abundance in my finances! In Jesus' precious name I pray, Amen.

SCRIPTURE REFERENCES

Deuteronomy 8:9, 18
Revelation 21:21
Psalm 24:1
Psalm 34:10

Psalm 23:1
2 Corinthians 5:17 NASB
Galatians 3:13

Deuteronomy 28:6, 8, 12–13 NLT
2 Corinthians 9:8

131 Freedom from Loneliness, Isolation

HEAVENLY FATHER, You said, "It is not good that man should be alone." You created us for fellowship and love. There are fifty-nine "one another" and "each other" commands in the New Testament. You told us not to forsake the assembling of ourselves together, and You sent Your disciples out two by two. You said,

"Woe to him who is alone when he falls, for he has no one to help him up. Again, if two lie down together, they will keep warm; but how can one be warm alone? Though one may be overpowered by another, two can withstand him. And a threefold cord is not quickly broken." Father, You meant for us to be in communion with others, especially other believers. Though everyone may have periods of isolation and loneliness, it's not Your will for us to camp there. Help me to come out of isolation and loneliness, even if it's uncomfortable at first. Help me to do my part to sow seeds of friendship and community so that I can develop meaningful, mutually beneficial relationships with others.

Father, if I have allowed hurts, rejections, and betrayals from others to make me retract into my shell, self-isolate, or put up walls around my heart, I ask You to heal my soul. Psalm 23:3 says that You restore my soul. Wash away all the pain by the blood of Jesus and remove the walls around my heart. Set me free from this self-imposed prison and help me to stop hiding and isolating. Help me to love others as though I've never been hurt and not be on guard with everybody. I pray that I would live a big, fulfilling life with meaningful relationships and community.

In the name of Jesus, I bind, break, cut off, cancel, and nullify every stronghold and spirit of loneliness, isolation, hiding, rejection, pain, and distrust from me. I command the protective walls around my heart to come down, in the name of Jesus. I speak healing, wholeness, restoration, and freedom to my soul, in the name of Jesus. Father, help me to enjoy amazing friendships, love, and community. Thank You that Your plans for me are good, and You are going to bring me out of this season of loneliness and isolation into a season of rich relationships and abundant life. In Jesus' name I pray, Amen.

SCRIPTURE REFERENCES

Genesis 2:18	Mark 6:7	Psalm 23:3
Hebrews 10:25	Ecclesiastes 4:10–12	Jeremiah 29:11

132 Freedom from Mental Torment, Suicidal Thoughts

HEAVENLY FATHER, I come to You asking for freedom from mental torment and suicidal thoughts. I repent for believing any lies, entertaining wrong thoughts and emotions, and engaging in any sins that opened the door to the enemy's attacks. I ask You to forgive me, wash me clean by the blood of Jesus, and close every door to the enemy. Your Word says, "Submit to God. Resist the devil and he will flee from you." I submit my mind, emotions, and everything in my life to You. I resist the devil, knowing that he must flee from me. Your Word says that You have not given me a spirit of fear, but of power, love, and a *sound mind*. So, give me a healthy, sound, peaceful mind, in Jesus' name. Let Your peace that surpasses all understanding guard my heart and mind through Christ Jesus. Help me to have the mind of Christ, take every thought captive, and reject every thought that doesn't line up with Your Word.

Father, thank You that Jesus came to set the captives free and proclaim liberty to those who are bound and oppressed. Whom the Son sets free is free indeed! So, I ask You to break every chain of mental torment and suicidal thoughts off me, in Jesus' mighty name. Jesus, You have given me authority over all the power of the enemy. The devil and his demons are subject to me in Your name. Whatever I bind on earth will be bound in heaven. So, I bind, rebuke, cut off, and cast out every tormenting spirit, spirit of suicide, lying spirit, spirit of oppression, fear, anxiety, depression, despair, hopelessness, and every demonic spirit from me, in the mighty name of Jesus. I cover my mind and every part of my being with the blood of Jesus. No weapon formed against me shall prosper.

Father, You said, "The Lord is faithful, who will establish you and guard you from the evil one." I ask You to guard me from the evil one. Put Your mighty hedge of protection around me and my mind that the enemy cannot penetrate. I cover my mind with the blood of Jesus and cast down every lie, wrong thought, and argument that exalts itself against the knowledge of God in my life, in Jesus' name. Thank You, Lord, that I am free from mental torment and suicidal thoughts. I have a healthy, peaceful mind and think positive, faith-filled, victorious thoughts. I pray all these things in Jesus' precious name, Amen.

SCRIPTURE REFERENCES

James 4:7	Luke 4:18	Revelation 12:11
2 Timothy 1:7	Galatians 5:1	Isaiah 54:17
Philippians 4:7	John 8:36	2 Thessalonians 3:3
1 Corinthians 2:16	Luke 10:17, 19	Job 1:10
2 Corinthians 10:4–5	Matthew 18:18	

133 Freedom from Negativity

HEAVENLY FATHER, I come to You asking to be set free from negativity. Thank You that Jesus came to set me free from all captivity and oppression. Whom the Son sets free is free indeed! I don't want to be held captive or oppressed by negativity anymore. I want to be free from everything that is a stumbling block in my life. So, I ask You to break every chain of negativity off me, in Jesus' name. Your Word says, "Be imitators of God as dear children." You're not a negative, sour, cynical God but a positive, loving, gracious God. Help me to imitate You as Your child and representative on earth. Help me to be the fragrant aroma of Christ everywhere I go and not emit negative vibes but positive, uplifting vibes. Help me not to speak or write anything that is not positive and edifying.

Father, I repent for the sins of my ancestors that may have opened the door to a generational stronghold of negativity. I ask You to forgive every sin, iniquity, and transgression of my ancestors and cleanse my family line by the blood of Jesus. You said, "If anyone is in Christ, he is a new creation; old things have passed away; behold, all things have become new." Thank You that I have a new bloodline and lineage in Christ Jesus, and every generational curse has passed away. Jesus has redeemed me from every curse. I break, cut off, renounce, revoke, and nullify every generational curse of negativity, in Jesus' mighty name! The weapons of my warfare are not carnal but mighty in God for the pulling down of strongholds and casting down arguments and every high thing that exalts itself against the knowledge of God. So, in the name of Jesus, I pull down, demolish, and shatter the stronghold of negativity! I command the spirit of negativity to leave me now and never come back, in Jesus' name! I cast down every negative thought in my mind and cover my mind and thoughts with the blood of Jesus.

Father, help me to be transformed by the renewing of my mind. Train me to focus on the good in life, the world, and people, rather than the bad. Help me to have a victorious mindset and only think on things that are positive, faith-filled, victorious, and worthy of praise. Thank You that I am free from negativity forever and I will be known as a positive, can-do, faith-filled person. I pray all these things in the precious name of Jesus, Amen.

SCRIPTURE REFERENCES

Luke 4:18	Ephesians 4:29	2 Corinthians 10:4-6
John 8:36	2 Corinthians 5:17	Romans 12:2
Ephesians 5:1	Galatians 3:13	Philippians 4:8

134 Freedom from Panic Attacks

Heavenly Father, I come to You asking for freedom from panic attacks. I repent for anything I have done, thought, or said that opened the door to the enemy and gave him legal access to attack me. I ask You to forgive me, wash me clean by the blood of Jesus, and close every door to the enemy. Your Word says, "Submit to God. Resist the devil and he will flee from you." I submit my mind, emotions, and everything in my life to You, and I resist the devil, knowing that he must flee from me. You have not given me a spirit of fear but of power, love, and a sound mind. So, give me a healthy, sound, peaceful mind, in Jesus' name. Let Your peace that surpasses all understanding guard my heart and mind through Christ Jesus. Help me to have the mind of Christ, take every thought captive, and reject every thought that doesn't line up with Your Word.

Father, thank You that Jesus came to set the captives free and proclaim liberty to those who are bound and oppressed. Whom the Son sets free is free indeed! So, I ask You to break every chain of panic attacks off me, in Jesus' mighty name. Jesus, You have given me authority over all the power of the enemy. The devil and his demons are subject to me in Your name. Whatever I bind on earth will be bound in heaven. I bind, rebuke, cut off, and cast out every spirit of panic attacks, fear, anxiety, torment, and every demonic spirit from me, in the mighty name of Jesus. I cover my mind and every part of my being with the blood of Jesus. No weapon formed against me shall prosper.

Father, You said, "The Lord is faithful, who will establish you and guard you from the evil one." I ask You to guard me from the evil one. Put Your mighty hedge of protection around me and my mind that the enemy cannot penetrate. I cover my mind with the blood of Jesus and cast down every lie, wrong thought, and argument that exalts itself against the knowledge of God in my life, in

Jesus' name. Thank You, Lord, that I am free from panic attacks. I will walk in the peace, freedom, and victory that Jesus died to give me. I pray all these things in Jesus' precious name, Amen.

SCRIPTURE REFERENCES

James 4:7	Luke 4:18	Revelation 12:11
2 Timothy 1:7	Galatians 5:1	Isaiah 54:17
Philippians 4:7	John 8:36	2 Thessalonians 3:3
1 Corinthians 2:16	Luke 10:17, 19	Job 1:10
2 Corinthians 10:4–5	Matthew 18:18	

---

135 Freedom from Pride

HEAVENLY FATHER, I come to You seeking freedom from pride. Your Word says that You hate evil, pride, and arrogance and that "pride goes before destruction." We are told that "God opposes the proud but shows favor to the humble." Pride is how Lucifer fell from heaven and became Satan. I repent for all the ways pride has manifested in my life. I repent for the times I thought I knew better or simply wanted my own way and acted independently and rebelliously toward You. I repent for the times I exalted my desires, needs, opinions, and agenda over others when Your Word says, "In humility value others above yourselves." I repent for the times I thought too highly of myself when Your Word says, "Do not think of yourself more highly than you ought." I ask You to forgive me, cleanse me of all unrighteousness, and deliver me from every form of pride. I ask for true, godly humility from the heart.

Father, I repent for the sins of my ancestors that may have opened the door to a generational stronghold of pride. I ask You to forgive every sin of my ancestors and cleanse my family line by the blood of Jesus. You said, "If anyone is in Christ, he is a new creation; old things have passed away; behold, all things have become new." Thank You that I have a new bloodline and lineage in Christ Jesus, and every generational curse has passed away. Jesus has redeemed me from every curse. I break, cut off, renounce, revoke, and nullify every generational curse of pride, in Jesus' mighty name! The weapons of my warfare are not carnal but mighty in God for the pulling down of strongholds. So, in the name of Jesus, I pull down, demolish, and shatter the stronghold of pride. I command the spirit of pride to leave me now and never come back, in Jesus' name!

Lord Jesus, You said, "Whoever exalts himself will be humbled, and he who humbles himself will be exalted." Your Word tells us that humility unleashes a multitude of God's blessings, including an abundance of peace, increased joy, God's wisdom, riches, honor, life, and God's favor. Help me to reject pride and walk humbly before You and all people so that I can represent You well, enjoy the fullness of Your blessings, and become all You created me to be. I pray all these things in the precious name of Jesus, Amen.

SCRIPTURE REFERENCES

Proverbs 8:13	Romans 12:3 NIV	Isaiah 29:19
Proverbs 16:18	2 Corinthians 5:17	Proverbs 11:2
James 4:6 NIV	Matthew 23:12	Proverbs 22:4
Philippians 2:3 NIV	Psalm 37:11	

136 Freedom from Procrastination

HEAVENLY FATHER, I come to You asking to be delivered from all procrastination. Thank You that Jesus came to set me free from all captivity. Whom the Son sets free is free indeed. I don't want to be held captive by procrastination anymore. I want to be free from everything that is a stumbling block in my life. So, I ask You to break every chain of procrastination off me, in Jesus' name. Your Word tells us to "walk circumspectly, not as fools but as wise, redeeming the time, because the days are evil." Help me to redeem the time and not put off or avoid things I need to take care of. Give me an excellent spirit to stay on top of my business and be a good steward of all my affairs. Help me not to procrastinate out of fear, but to have the courage to face things that may be difficult or unpleasant and the faith to step out and do what You've put in my heart to do. Your Word says that You have not given me a spirit of fear, but of power, love, and a sound mind. So, help me to be fearless, full of faith, and to never allow fear, laziness, or anything else to cause me to procrastinate.

Father, help me to understand that when I feel a tug in my spirit to do something, there is a window of grace and anointing to do what You are prompting me to do. After that window closes, I won't have the same grace and anointing to do it. In some cases, I may even miss out on an opportunity or blessing. So, help me to be quick to act on the promptings of Your Spirit and conquer procrastination once and for all in my life.

Thank You that the weapons of my warfare are not carnal but mighty in God for the pulling down of strongholds. So, in the name of Jesus, I pull down, demolish, and shatter the stronghold of procrastination. I bind, rebuke, and cast out every spirit of procrastination, fear, laziness, and avoidance from me, in Jesus' name. Father, thank You that I am free from procrastination and that I will step into new levels of victory, favor, and destiny. I pray all these things in the precious name of Jesus, Amen.

SCRIPTURE REFERENCES

John 8:36	2 Timothy 1:7	Luke 10:19
Ephesians 5:15–16	2 Corinthians 10:4	Matthew 18:18

137 Freedom from Selfishness

Heavenly Father, I come to You seeking freedom from selfishness. I repent from selfishness and putting my own desires, needs, and agenda before others. I ask You to forgive me, cleanse me of all unrighteousness, and deliver me from selfishness. Your Word says, "In humility consider others as more important than yourselves," and "No one should seek their own good, but the good of others." Jesus said, "It is more blessed to give than to receive." Help me to understand that my life will be so much more blessed and fulfilling when I let go of selfishness and put others first. Help me to take myself off the throne, get myself off my mind, and live "others minded."

Father, let me live by Jesus' words: "Whoever would be great among you must be your servant, and whoever would be first among you must be slave of all. For even the Son of Man came not to be served but to serve, and to give his life as a ransom for many." Give me a servant's heart and mindset like Jesus, who washed His disciples' dirty feet and gave His life to serve mankind. Proverbs 11:25 says, "A generous person will prosper; whoever refreshes others will be refreshed." Help me to live a lifestyle that refreshes and blesses others with generous love, kindness, encouragement, finances, and service. I pray that I would not love in word only but in deed and selfless sacrifice for others.

Father, You said the weapons of my warfare are not carnal but mighty in God for pulling down strongholds. So, in the name of Jesus, I pull down, demolish, and shatter the stronghold of selfishness and pride. I command the spirits of selfishness and pride to leave me now and never come back, in Jesus' name! Lord, thank You for delivering me from selfishness and pride and transforming me into a selfless, Christlike servant who puts others first. I pray all these things in Jesus' precious name, Amen.

SCRIPTURE REFERENCES

Philippians 2:3 CSB
1 Corinthians 10:24 NIV
Philippians 2:4
Acts 20:35 NIV
Mark 10:43–45 ESV
Proverbs 11:25 NIV
1 John 3:18
2 Corinthians 10:4

138 Freedom from Self-Pity, Victim Spirit

HEAVENLY FATHER, I come to You asking to be set free from self-pity and a victim spirit. I repent for entertaining self-pity and victimhood when Your Word says that in all things I am more than a conqueror, that You always cause me to triumph in Christ Jesus, and that I have the victory in Jesus. I ask You to forgive me, cleanse me by the blood of Jesus, and close every door to the enemy. Help me to live with a victorious mindset and reject any self-pity and victim thoughts. I am a victor, not a victim!

Father, I repent for the sins of my ancestors that may have opened the door to self-pity and a victim spirit. I ask You to forgive every sin, iniquity, and transgression of my ancestors and cleanse my family line by the blood of Jesus. You said, "If anyone is in Christ, he is a new creation; old things have passed away; behold, all things have come new." Thank You that I have a new bloodline and lineage in Christ Jesus, and every generational curse has passed away. Jesus has redeemed me from every curse. I break, cut off, renounce, revoke, and nullify every generational curse of self-pity and victimhood, in Jesus' mighty name! The weapons of my warfare are not carnal but mighty in God for pulling down strongholds and casting down arguments and every high thing that exalts itself against the knowledge of God. So, in the name of Jesus, I pull down, demolish, and shatter the stronghold of self-pity and victimhood! I command the spirit of self-pity and being a victim to leave me now and never come back, in Jesus' name! I cast down every lie in my mind that I am a victim, that God has somehow forsaken me, and every "woe is me," self-pity thought, in the name of Jesus!

Father, help me to be transformed by the renewing of my mind. Help me to study what Your Word says about me and mediate on that instead of the lies of the enemy or my errant thoughts. Train me to have a victorious mindset and only think on things that are positive, faith-filled, victorious, and worthy of praise. Thank You that Jesus came to set me free from all captivity and oppression and I am free from self-pity and a victim spirit forever. I pray all these things in the precious name of Jesus, Amen.

SCRIPTURE REFERENCES

Romans 8:37	2 Corinthians 5:17	Romans 12:2
2 Corinthians 2:14	Galatians 3:13	Philippians 4:8
1 Corinthians 15:57	2 Corinthians 10:4-6	Luke 4:18

139 Freedom from Self-Sabotage

HEAVENLY FATHER, I come to You asking for freedom from self-sabotage. Thank You that Jesus came to set me free from all captivity and everything that is a stumbling block in my life. Whom the Son sets free is free indeed! I ask You to break every chain of self-sabotage off me, in Jesus' mighty name. Father, You are always for me and never against me. Help me not to be against myself. Help me to love myself, believe in myself, and be for myself. Heal my soul from any damage, and deliver me from lies I have believed that cause me to self-sabotage. Set me free from any wrong belief that I don't deserve happiness or success, fear of success, self-doubt, self-loathing, or any other root of self-sabotage. Help me not to do things and communicate in ways that undermine myself.

The apostle Paul wrote, "I do not understand what I do. For what I want to do I do not do, but what I hate I do. . . . Thanks be to God, who delivers me through Jesus Christ our Lord!" Thank You that You will deliver me from all self-sabotaging thinking, decisions, behavior, and communication. Father, You said, "If any of you lacks wisdom, you should ask God, who gives generously to all without finding fault, and it will be given to you." I ask for the wisdom and self-awareness to see, understand, and overcome my patterns of self-sabotage with Your help.

Lord, thank You that "the weapons of our warfare are not carnal but mighty in God for pulling down strongholds, casting down arguments and every high thing that exalts itself against the knowledge of God." So, in the name of Jesus, I pull down, demolish, and shatter the stronghold of self-sabotage! I bind, rebuke, cut off, and cast out every spirit of fear, self-sabotage, lying, self-loathing and self-doubt, and every demonic spirit that causes me to self-sabotage, in the name of Jesus! I cast down every lie, wrong belief, and argument that causes me to self-sabotage, in Jesus' name. Father, thank You for setting me free from self-sabotage and helping me get into agreement with Your thoughts about me and vision for my life. Thank You that I will become all You created me to be and live my best life for Your glory. In Jesus' name I pray, Amen.

SCRIPTURE REFERENCES

Luke 4:18	Romans 7:15–25 NIV	2 Corinthians 10:4–5
John 8:36	James 1:5 NIV	

140 Freedom from Sexual Immorality

Heavenly Father, I come to You repenting for sexual immorality, specifically [name the sin(s)—lust, pornography, fornication, masturbation, adultery, perversion, etc.]. I have violated Your commands to "be holy, for [You] are holy," "flee from sexual immorality," and "put to death . . . sexual immorality, impurity, passion, evil desire." I have sinned against You, my own body, and [if you have one] my wife/husband. Your Word says that if I confess my sins to You, You are faithful and just to forgive me and cleanse me of all unrighteousness. I ask You to forgive me, wash me clean by the blood of Jesus, and close every door to the enemy. Thank You that Jesus came to set me free from all captivity and oppression. Whom the Son sets free is free indeed. I don't want to be held captive or oppressed by sexual immorality anymore. I ask You to break every chain of sexual immorality off me and set me free, in Jesus' name. Help me to offer my body as a living sacrifice, holy and pleasing to You, which is my true and proper worship. Help me to control my own body in holiness and honor and not be overcome by lust like those who don't know You.

Father, I repent for the sins of my ancestors that may have opened the door to a generational stronghold of [name the stronghold(s)]. I ask You to forgive every sin, iniquity, and transgression of my ancestors and cleanse my family line by the blood of Jesus. You said, "If anyone is in Christ, he is a new creation; old things have passed away; behold, all things have become new." Thank You that I have a new bloodline and lineage in Christ Jesus, and every generational curse has passed away. Jesus has redeemed me from every curse. I break, cut off, renounce, revoke, and nullify every generational curse of sexual immorality, in Jesus' mighty name! The weapons of my warfare are not carnal but mighty in God for the pulling down of strongholds. So, in the name of Jesus, I pull down, demolish, and shatter the stronghold of sexual immorality.

I command every spirit of lust, perversion, pornography, fornication, adultery, masturbation, seduction, and every spirit of sexual immorality to leave me now and never come back, and I cut off, renounce, and revoke every agreement and association with you, in the name of Jesus!

Father, Your Word says, "Don't copy the behavior and customs of this world, but let God transform you into a new person by changing the way you think." Help me not to have anything in common with the world's wicked ways but to be set apart and holy. Transform me into a new person. Make me an authentic, pure follower of Jesus so that I can make You proud, represent You well, and become all You created me to be. Paul tells us, "God is faithful, and he will not let you be tempted beyond your ability, but with the temptation he will also provide the way of escape, that you may be able to endure it." Help me to resist temptation and take the way of escape before I am ensnared. Thank You for setting me free from sexual immorality and helping me walk in freedom for the rest of my life. I pray all these things in Jesus' name, Amen.

SCRIPTURE REFERENCES

1 Peter 1:16	Romans 12:1	Romans 12:2 NLT
1 Corinthians 6:18 ESV	1 Thessalonians 4:3-5	1 Corinthians 10:13 ESV
Colossians 3:5 ESV	2 Corinthians 5:17	
1 John 1:9	Galatians 3:13	
John 8:36	2 Corinthians 10:4-6	

141 Prayer to Break Generational Curses

FATHER, I repent for the sins of all my ancestors on the sides of both my father and mother, going all the way back to Adam and Eve, which brought a generational curse on my family line. I repent for my own participation in those sins. I specifically repent for the generational sin(s) of [name the sin patterns you have observed in yourself and your recent ancestors—anger, addictions, pride, etc.] I ask You to forgive me and my ancestors of every sin and cleanse my entire family line by the sanctifying, delivering blood of Jesus. Your Word says that Jesus became a curse for me by hanging on a tree and redeemed me from every curse. You said, "If anyone is in Christ, he is a new creation; old things have passed away; behold, all things have become new." Thank You that I have a new bloodline and lineage in Christ Jesus, and every generational curse has passed away. I break, sever, renounce, revoke, and nullify every generational curse off me and my descendants, in Jesus' mighty name. I declare that every generational curse in my family line ends with me and will not be passed down to my descendants. I am setting a new legacy for my family and future generations.

Thank You that Jesus came "to proclaim freedom to the captives and . . . to set free the oppressed." "For freedom, Christ set [me and my descendants] free." Your Word also tells us, "If the Son sets you free, you will be free indeed." By faith, I receive the freedom that Jesus died to give me from every generational curse. Jesus, You gave me authority over all the power of the enemy. The devil and his demons are subject to me in Your name. Whatever I bind on earth will be bound in heaven. So, I bind, rebuke, cut off, and cast out every demonic spirit associated with generational curses in me and my family, in Jesus' name. I command you to go from me and my descendants and never come back, in Jesus' name. I cover myself and my descendants with the blood of Jesus and declare that we are free and victorious in Christ. No curse can operate in our lives, in Jesus' name. I pray all these things in the matchless name of Jesus, Amen.

SCRIPTURE REFERENCES

Galatians 3:13 NLT	Galatians 5:1 CSB	Matthew 18:18
2 Corinthians 5:17	John 8:36 ESV	Revelation 12:11
Luke 4:18 HCSB	Luke 10:17, 19	

142 Prayer to Break Word Curses

HEAVENLY FATHER, thank You that Galatians 3:13 says that Jesus became a curse for me at the cross and redeemed me from every curse. Thank You that I am free from every spoken curse, generational curse, or any other curse by the shed blood of Jesus. You tell us that "like a fluttering sparrow or a darting swallow, an undeserved curse will not land on its intended victim." No curse anyone tries to speak over me or put on me will stick because I am purchased, redeemed, and covered by the blood of the Lamb. When the Moabite king Balak asked the prophet Balaam to speak a curse over Israel, Balaam said, "How can I curse those whom God has not cursed? How can I condemn those whom the Lord has not condemned?" Thank You that no one can speak a curse over me because You have not cursed or condemned me. You call me blessed, highly favored, and a masterpiece.

In the name of Jesus, I bind, break, cancel, and nullify every word curse spoken over me. I command every negative word that's ever been spoken over me by my parents, family members, friends, coaches, teachers, doctors, or anyone else to fall to the ground and have no effect, in Jesus' name. Father, I ask You to heal and restore my soul from the hurt caused by those negative words. Help me to forgive the people who spoke those words and release them and the pain they caused to You. I ask for Your Holy Spirit who lives inside of me to erase those negative words from my memory and subconscious. I pray I would have no memory or thought of them again, and it would be as though they had never been spoken.

Lord, I repent for allowing the words of others to haunt me, alter my self-image, and diminish my self-esteem. Your Word tells us to "be transformed by the renewing of your mind." Help me to renew my mind daily with Your Word, believe only what You say about me, and reject any words to the contrary. Help me to walk confidently in my identity in Christ and have a godly self-image and self-esteem that align with Your Word. Thank You that I can live free and victorious because You love, approve, and accept me unconditionally. I pray all these things in the precious name of Jesus, Amen.

SCRIPTURE REFERENCES

Galatians 3:13
Proverbs 26:2 NLT
Numbers 23:8 NLT
Psalm 23:3
Romans 12:2

143 Prayer to Break Soul Ties

HEAVENLY FATHER, I humble myself before You and surrender every area of my life to You. Thank You that 1 John 1:9 says that when we confess our sins to You, You are faithful and just to forgive our sins and cleanse us of all unrighteousness. I confess that I have had relationships and associations in the past that were unholy, transgressed Your will, and did not glorify You. I repent for every sexual relationship I had outside of the covenant of marriage when Your Word clearly prohibits sex outside of marriage. I repent for every relationship, friendship, and association that transgressed Your Word or did not glorify You. I ask You to forgive me and cleanse me of all unrighteousness by the blood of Jesus.

I break, renounce, revoke, and sever every unholy soul tie between me and [name specific people you know you formed unholy soul ties with] and anyone else I formed unholy soul ties with, whether living or dead, sexual or nonsexual, and I command every demonic spirit associated with those soul ties to leave me and never come back, in Jesus' name.

Father, thank You that I am free in Christ Jesus from every unholy and unhealthy soul tie. Thank You that I am forgiven and cleansed by the blood of the Lamb. I ask You to heal and restore my soul from the damage caused by these unholy and unhealthy relationships, and help me only to have healthy, God-glorifying relationships from now on. I pray all these things in the delivering, healing, cleansing, restoring name of the Lord Jesus Christ, Amen.

SCRIPTURE REFERENCES

1 John 1:9	1 Samuel 18:1	Proverbs 6:32
Genesis 2:24	2 Corinthians 6:14, 16	

STEVE AUSTIN is a former attorney, a *USA Today* bestselling author, and a pastor at Lakewood Church in Houston, Texas, for over twenty years. With a passion for ministering to the sick, Steve has ministered to thousands of patients in the world's largest medical center—the Texas Medical Center in Houston. He is the founder and president of Living Hope Chaplaincy, a 501c3 nonprofit organization that recruits, trains, and places volunteers in hospitals to provide spiritual care. Steve is a powerful prayer warrior who has taught and written about prayer for thirty years.

CONNECT WITH STEVE

PastorSteveAustin.com
LivingHopeChaplaincy.org

- Steve Austin
- @PastorSteveAustin
- @PastorSteveAustin
- @PastorSteve1
- @PastorSteve7777